IN LITERATURE

Paul O'Flinn

Pluto Press

First published 1975 by Pluto Press Limited
Unit 10, Spencer Court, 7 Chalcot Road, London NW1 8LH
Copyright © Pluto Press 1975

ISBN 0 902818 89 9

Printed by C. Nicholls & Company Ltd
The Philips Park Press, Manchester
Designed by Richard Hollis, GrR
Cover photographs by Lance Hodgson

CONTENTS

INTRODUCTION

A lot of recent Marxist writing about literature seems to me to be inaccessible and boring. This book is meant to be Marxist but I've tried to make it accessible and not boring.

1. WILLIAM GOLDING AND ORIGINAL SIN

William Golding's *Lord of the Flies* is one of the most influential post-war novels. First published in 1954, it caught on in a couple of years and by the end of the decade Penguins could scarcely print it fast enough. It was made into a reasonably successful film and soon found itself required reading in school syllabuses all over the world. *Lord of the Flies*, it's generally agreed, is a modern classic.

What's it about? If it's a while since you saw the film or read the book it's worth recalling the story. It's set in a future of atomic war with 'the reds' as the enemy. A party of English private schoolboys, ages ranging from six to twelve, are being evacuated when their plane is shot down over the Pacific. They climb out of the crash to find themselves on a desert island paradise – coral reef, palm trees, lagoon, the lot. The rest of the story is about how this paradise is turned into hell by the nature of the boys themselves. Discipline starts to break down. A few   Ralph, Piggy, Simon – try to maintain standards but the majority end up following the vicious Jack, end up, in Piggy's phrase, like 'a pack of painted niggers'. Simon is ritually slaughtered and Piggy is pushed off a cliff. Next there's a savage manhunt: Jack and his mob chase Ralph across the island, reducing it to a blazing wreckage with fires designed to smoke Ralph out. But help is on the way. The flames have attracted the British Navy. The book closes with the boys in tears at the feet of a puzzled officer and a group of ratings who have landed to see what the trouble is.

So far so good. Golding has selected and isolated some middle-class private school boys, has put them under a microscope and has decided that they are on the whole a vicious and nasty lot. The rest of us are sorry to hear this about the middle classes and hope they soon get better because in small but occasionally worthy ways they have something to contribute.

Perhaps it's not true, perhaps they aren't such a loathsome and vicious mob as Golding makes out. And yet he's uniquely well qualified to judge: four years at Oxford University, five years as an officer in the navy during the War, then twenty years as a grammar school teacher – more or less a lifetime spent almost exclusively in the company of middle-class males of all ages. Golding should know, and if he says they are a heap of crap, so be it. Certainly it's a verdict that one has heard repeated from time to time by disgruntled foreigners, Marxists, members of the British working classes and the like.

But what's this? James R. Baker claims that the purpose of *Lord of the Flies* 'was to show that the perennially repeated fall of man is caused by defects inherent in his own nature'.[1] William Golding agrees, and says that the book's aim is 'to trace the defects of society back to the defects of human nature'.[2]

So here we are at the heart of the matter. It's not just British middle-class males who are rubbish, it's everybody, it's human nature, says the novel and its author. That's why our fall is 'perennially repeated' and that's why any of us would reduce a paradise to a flaming hell in a couple of hundred pages. In short, as Bernard S. Oldsey and Stanley Weintraub put it, 'Golding writes . . . with the eyes of someone who has seen the Empire crumble and witnessed twentieth century manifestations of Original Sin'.[3] Amen.

How do we respond to dismal pieties of this sort? Respond to them we must, because if Golding is right and if what destroys all attempts to create and maintain a decent society is 'the darkness of man's heart', as the novel's last page has it, then we might as well pack away our socialist illusions, go home and pray.

Argument of this sort withers away once we stop for a moment and look at our actual situation. I wrote this book, a compositor set up the type, you are reading it. That means that the three of us are literate, something that probably wasn't true of our ancestors, say, a hundred and fifty years ago. Then again, the fact that I have time and money to sit and write this book and you have money to buy it and time to read it means that the pair of us are not fully occupied in struggling for the bare necessities of food, clothing and shelter – again, something not true of many of our ancestors. Or take the mere fact that you and I and the compositor are alive and yet as children we all had measles, flu, chickenpox and so on. The odds are that in any generation before today's one or more of us would have died from one of those childhood ailments. So in all sorts of small and not so small ways humanity has progressed, we have evolved and moved forward, we are not perennially condemned to trip up and remain stuck in the same groove.

Reactionaries, of course, can handle this line fairly easily. Ah yes, they explain patiently, agreed that the *quantity* of life has improved, that *materially* we're better off. But what about Standards? What about the *Quality of Life*? As Golding himself puts it, boys nowadays 'will have a far less brutish life than their nineteenth century ancestors, no doubt. They will believe less and fear less. But just as good money drives out bad so inferior culture drives out superior.'[4]

At the risk of sounding repetitive, the very fact that William Golding is able to raise the question of the decline of superior cultural standards, and that you and I and the compositor can eavesdrop on his complaint, is evidence of immense progress. Formerly, you'd have been illiterate, I'd have been a serf and the compositor would have been dead, so none of the three of us would have given a twopenny damn about declining cultural standards. Now we know it's an issue, we've the leisure to contemplate that fact and can, if we agree with Golding's analysis and have nothing important to do, busy ourselves about superior cultural standards (need for raising of).

But setting aside the whole question of whether superior culture has collapsed or not, there is nonetheless a clear contradiction in the unchanging human nature brigade's claim that it *has* collapsed. Either human nature is fixed and unchanging, in which case it will tend broadly to reproduce itself and its conditions unchanged over generations, or human nature is ever-shifting, ever-evolving, in which case it will constantly be caught up in remaking, revolutionising, wrecking and rebuilding itself and its conditions, its culture and its habits. Human nature and the culture that nature generates either stays the same or it doesn't. You can't have it both ways. You can't insist that human nature is always the same and muse on about the eternal darkness of man's heart, and then with the next breath write articles for the *Times Literary Supplement* complaining about the way things are changing and getting worse.

The root of contradictions of this sort is the fact that the 'human nature' argument is not so much truth as ideology – a conscious or unconscious attempt, that is, by a group or its spokesmen to interpret the world in terms that justify and sustain that group and its interests. What we are offered is not the real world but rather the illusions and fears of a class about that world. Hence the contradictions.

Take another example of contradictions of this sort in *Lord of the Flies*. Two children are playing on the island's beach:

Roger stooped, picked up a stone, aimed, and threw it at Henry – threw it to miss. The stone, that token of preposterous time, bounced five yards to Henry's right and fell in the water. Roger gathered a handful of stones and began to throw them. Yet there was a space round Henry, perhaps six yards in diameter, into which he dare not throw. Here, invisible yet strong, was the taboo of the old life. Round the squatting child was the protection of parents and school and policemen and the law. Roger's arm was conditioned by a civilization that knew nothing of him and was in ruins.

Penguin 1960, p.59.

Left to ourselves, this paragraph suggests, we'd naturally throw bricks at each other. We don't because there are various authority figures, thank Heavens, who tell us not to. Take them away and chaos follows, as the novel fully illustrates.

The problem here is that if it's human nature to chuck bricks at other people, chucking bricks at other people would not be confined to Roger but is something that the various authority figures – parents, schoolteachers, policemen – would enjoy doing too. But authority figures it seems are by and large exempt from the dark, awful, obscene, violent, greedy promptings of nature that the rest of us are liable to.

Human nature, in short, is something that ordinary people have very badly – which is why we need tough laws about strikes and why a spell of discipline in the Forces would do them all a power of good. Human nature, dark, awful, obscene, violent and greedy, is however not something that, say, Margaret Thatcher, Sir Alec Douglas Home, the Queen Mother and your friendly neighbourhood bobby have at all, and you can be thrown out of Conservative Association meetings for suggesting otherwise.

A last example from this sad but in important ways significant book. One aspect of 'the darkness of man's heart' that Golding presents is child beating. Jack's first action in power is described by his companion, Robert:

'He's going to beat Wilfred.'
'What for?'
Robert shook his head doubtfully.

'I don't know. He didn't say. He got angry and made us tie Wilfred up. He's been' – he giggled excitedly – 'he's been tied for hours, waiting –'

p.151.

Beating little boys' bottoms and deriving a furtive sexual pleasure from the prospect (note that Robert 'giggled excitedly') has absolutely nothing to do with human nature but has a lot to do with the morbid pressures generated by the English education system. It's a practice that's unknown in many other cultures. Take, for example, the Cheyenne Indians of the North American High Plains and you'll find no child beating whatsoever. This is not because of some superior moral quality in the Cheyennes but because, in a tiny tribe in a hostile environment, children are greatly loved and valued as insurance for the future and it therefore doesn't occur to people to hit them.

Views about hitting people in our own culture are a curious muddle. Thus a glance at the papers will show you that it's regarded as very wrong to beat up babies.

BATTERED BABIES TRAGEDY
NEW SHOCK PROBE SLAMS MONSTER PARENTS

the *Sun* might confide one morning. And yet it seems that at a certain age – two? four? six? – suddenly a damn good hiding never did anyone any harm, while the *Sun*'s sports pages will probably tell you that a stiff birching would soon sort out the soccer hooligans. And then apparently at a later age – twenty? twenty five? thirty? – it's no longer possible to pass messages through the buttocks to the conscience, so that you never see editorial writers calling for a sound thrashing for older delinquents like Lord Lambton and Richard Nixon.

Enough of the contradictions in the flagellation fantasies of British journalists. The point, to get back to *Lord of the Flies*, is that here as elsewhere what is presented as eternal, as a part of human nature, is in fact only temporary, a feature of the customs and beliefs of our own dearly beloved ruling classes. These customs and beliefs, as Golding magnificently portrays, are in important ways brutal, anti-life, dehumanising and degrading. The response of Golding and his fans is to fall on their knees before the everlasting horror of Man's Original Sin. We reject extreme solutions of this sort. Our response is much more moderate and sensible. We become revolutionary socialists.

---

[1] *William Golding: a Critical Study*, New York 1965, p.62.

[2] Quoted by E.L.Epstein, 'Notes on *Lord of the Flies*', in *Lord of the Flies*, New York 1959, p.250.

[3] *The Art of William Golding*, Bloomington 1968, p.38.

[4] 'On the Crest of the Wave', *Times Literary Supplement*, June 17, 1960.

2. ANIMAL FARM, 1984 AND SOCIALIST REVOLUTION

'Orwell? Yeah, we read a couple of his books at school. Really great. He's the bloke who showed that revolution couldn't work – all it means is going round in circles, swopping one lot of bosses for another – you know: "Big Brother's watching you". Because you can't change human nature, you see. There'll always be those on top and the mugs underneath, always has been and always will be: "All animals are equal but some animals are more equal than others".'

Everyone's come across this argument in various forms. Orwell's phrases have dropped into everyday speech and everyday newspaper editorials to become, as Isaac Deutscher put it, 'an ideological super weapon in the cold war'. Keep your nose clean, pay your bills and when you hear some hairy half-wit going on about socialism, look up from your *Daily Express* and shout '1984!' at him. Soon shut the blighter up.

And yet Orwell claimed shortly after the publication of *Animal Farm* that he wrote '*for* democratic Socialism'; and shortly after the publication of *1984* he insisted: 'My recent novel is NOT intended as an attack on Socialism . . .' (See *Collected Essays, Journalism and Letters of George Orwell*, London 1968, Vol. I, p.5 and Vol. IV, p.502).

So what are we to make of this socialist who for the past generation has supplied the Right with a whole armoury of blunt instruments with which to attack the Left? More important, what's useful in Orwell's ideas and Orwell's warnings for the present generation of socialists?

One way of starting to answer these questions is to have a look at some dates:

1903: Orwell born.

1926: General Strike defeated.

1927: September: Orwell decides to resign from the Indian Imperial Police.

October: Trotsky expelled from the Communist Party of the Soviet Union.

1929: Wall Street crash, unemployment starts to soar.

1936: July: Spanish Civil War begins.

December: Orwell to Spain – enlists in th militia of the semi-Trotskyist POUM (Partido Obrero de Unificacion Marxista).

1937: March: *Road to Wigan Pier* published.

June: POUM declared illegal by the Spanish Government – Orwell flees from Communist-organised purge in Barcelona.

1939–1945: Second World War.

1945: *Animal Farm* published.

1947: Orwell's tuberculosis diagnosed.

1949: *1984* published.

1950: Orwell dies.

1953: Stalin dies.

Briefly the point here is that, after police work in Burma, Orwell coincidentally shifted to the Left and decided to leave the police just a few weeks before Trotsky's expulsion from the Communist Party – an expulsion that marks a decisive tightening of Stalin's hold on what had been the crucial revolutionary movement. And then, a generation later, Orwell died three years before Stalin. In other words his life as a socialist matches almost exactly the era of Stalinist domination and frustration of revolutionary hopes. In Barcelona he had vivid and embittering personal experience of that domination and frustration. His work therefore stands as a direct reflection of that generation of despair.

More than that: his life as a socialist also coincides almost exactly with an era of defeat for the British working-class movement. The loss of the General Strike in 1926 was deeply demoralizing: trade-union membership, over eight million in the years before 1926, was nearly halved in the years that followed and didn't recover properly till the eve of Orwell's death. The number of working days spent on strike in the nineteen thirties and forties was often as low as ten per cent of the peak in the early twenties. Mass unemployment in the thirties was a further blow, and the apathy and depression that this battering induced in sections of the working class is sharply recorded by Orwell in *The Road to Wigan Pier*.

In short what we have here is not St.George who taught us abiding moral truths about Human Nature and Revolution as it was in the beginning, is now and ever shall be, but rather a writer theorising gloomily out of the centre of a period of combined and interconnected Stalinist stranglehold and broken working-class militancy. All that is now changed. The Stalinist monopoly is broken and not many would accuse, say, the miners of being insufficiently militant. What then is left of Orwell's analysis?

However, the problem that remains with *Animal Farm* is that it's a *fable* and can therefore be directed at any revolution. It presents itself not as a direct attack on Stalinism but rather as a parable about the necessary failure of revolutions. This is indeed how a generation since 1945 have been encouraged to read it. But this is far from Orwell's intentions as spelled out by him in the Preface to the Ukrainian edition of *Animal Farm*:

> Indeed, in my opinion, nothing has contributed so much to the corruption of the original idea of Socialism as the belief that Russia is a Socialist country and that every act of its rulers must be excused, if not imitated.

16

> And so for the past ten years I have been convinced that the destruction of the Soviet myth was essential if we wanted a revival of the Socialist movement.
>
> *op cit*, Vol. III, p.405.

The publishers who turned down *Animal Farm* were quite clear that what they were being offered was an attack not on socialism or on revolution but on Stalinism. Victor Gollancz remarked: 'We couldn't have published it then. Those people (the Russians) were fighting for us and had just saved our necks at Stalingrad.' Jonathan Cape also rejected *Animal Farm*, telling Orwell that after consulting the Ministry of Information, he realised that:

> it might be regarded as something which it was highly ill-advised to publish at the present time. If the fable were addressed generally to dictators and dictatorships at large then publication would be all right, but the fable does follow, as I now see, so completely the progress of the Russian Soviets and their two dictators, that it can apply only to Russia, to the exclusion of the other dictatorships.
>
> Quoted in George Orwell, 'The Freedom of the Press',
> *Times Literary Supplement*, Sept. 15, 1972.

The Soviet Union was then an ally, so direct assaults on Stalinism were not on. Orwell did it indirectly, through a thinly disguised fable. Indeed he had to – it was either that or no publication. Even so four publishers still refused to handle it before Secker and Warburg finally agreed to take it.

And then the world changed. The Second World War ended in 1945, the Cold War began and by 1946 *Animal Farm* was a bestseller. The capitalist party line had taken one of its frequent U-turns and Orwell from being 'highly ill-advised' and poor found himself U.S. Book of the Month Club choice and rich. And thus an attack on Stalinism, mounted in a veiled way because of historical circumstances, becomes, because of a sharp shift in those circumstances, an apparent attack on the whole notion of revolutionary change.

Two important points about *1984*. The first is that it projects uninterruptedly into the future all the negative tendencies Orwell saw around him in the nineteen forties. Winston Smith's London is very much forties London, blitzed, dirty and shortage-riddled, after forty more years of the same only more so. All the decaying freedoms and growing intrusions of the war and the post-war years are seized on and magnified in the novel. We need to argue against this version of the future that history doesn't work that way, with graphs moving ever upward or ever downward, with tendencies unfolding unchallenged. History is a dialectical process.

So what does that mean? Take a simple recent example. In 1971 no dockers went to prison but in that year the Conservative government passed a law limiting trade-union rights so that in 1972 five dockers landed in Penton-ville for organizing a picket. Projecting this trend we might say that by 1975 picketing would be extinct, 413 dockers would be in prison and holding a union card would be on the way to being a capital offence. In fact this is not so: the Industrial Relations Act has gone and, once again, no dockers are in prison. Why? Because several hundred thousand people went on strike and got the dockers out in less than a week. What happened was that men and women saw a trend developing that threatened them and their organizations and so acted decisively to halt it. Action of this kind is not allowed for in *1984*. The proles, after forty more passive years, are an apathetic, ignorant lump. They retain a certain potentially subversive life but for the most part they are, like Boxer in *Animal Farm*, hard working, thick and manipulated into slavery with laughable ease. But engineers know and have shown, dockers know and have shown, miners know and have shown, that such a picture is false.

18

The truth is that governments can design all sorts of sophisticated halters and handcuffs, can get them approved by Parliament and issued to judges and policemen. But if people don't like wearing them they can and do break them as soon as they are clapped on.

Orwell, then, is pessimistic about the possibility of direct working-class action to preserve and extend freedom. Part of the reason for this is that he lived in and so drew his experience from a period with the unique and shattering limitations outlined at the start of this chapter. But there's more to it than that, and this is the second important point about *1984*: it is that by the time he came to write it Orwell was a socialist with almost no contact with the socialist or working-class movement. Such a man is very vulnerable to the misconceptions that that kind of isolation can create.

There are various reasons for this isolation. In the thirties Orwell had been a member of the ILP (Independent Labour Party) but resigned shortly after the start of the Second World War when they took up a pacifist position. In 1943 he became literary editor of *Tribune*, the paper of the Labour Party left, and he remained a supporter of that group for the rest of his life. So we find him remarking in 1949: 'If only I could become Nye's (Aneurin Bevan's) *éminence grise* we'd soon have this country on its feet.' It's a curious and a giveaway thing for a socialist to say. Socialism, after all, is supposed to be about working-class action leading to full freedom, not the sort of cloak and-dagger manoeuvres by a tiny elite that this remark suggests. But the point is, where in 1949 was the socialist party to stir up and grow out of that sort of mass activity? The answer is nowhere. The Communist Party remained Stalinist and, as such and by definition, part of the problem rather than its solution. The Labour Party as usual had run out of nerve and ideas and was drifting towards electoral defeat. Other left alternatives were then undeveloped.

Add to this the fact that Orwell was by that date dying

of tuberculosis and the depressing picture is complete. Socialism in such a context becomes not a shared activity, sharpened at meetings, warmed in demonstrations, revised through conflicts, cheered by the occasional victory. Instead, it's a lonely dwindling faith, challenged every time you open a newspaper, switch on the radio, go to the cinema or overhear what Orwell called the 'constant bah-bahing' of those Tory voices passing to and fro in the private sanitoria where his tuberculosis took him. In such a context working-class action stops being something seen and tried with its possibilities realised and soberly estimated in day-to-day experience. It becomes a dim, half-forgotten doctrine over-whelmed by a sense of all the forces working against it. In such a context you write *1984*.

In the very different context of the seventies do *Animal Farm* and *1984* have anything left to offer? Obviously they do. Orwell knew that the future was not inevitably socialist as Fabians used to believe. He knew with Engels that there's a choice – socialism or barbarism. At a time when the working class seemed stalled and revolutionary organisations didn't exist barbarism seemed likeliest, so he wrote to warn. It's still a valid warning. Either we build the socialism that Orwell believed in or they build the 1984 that Orwell was afraid of.

3. FORSTER AND PERSONAL RELATIONSHIPS
or
She's Leaving Home for a Room with a View

The Beatles' *Sgt. Pepper's Lonely Hearts Club Band* was one of the best pop LPs in the past ten years. Part of its success lay in the way it captured some of the most powerful notions lying around in our society. One idea in particular comes up in several lyrics. In 'A Little Help from My Friends' there's:

> I just need somebody to love

and in 'Within You Without You' there's:

> With our love – we could save the world   if they only knew.
> Try to realise it's all within yourself.

Then there's this in 'She's Leaving Home':

> She's leaving home after living alone
> For so many years. Bye, Bye
> Friday morning at nine o'clock she is far away
> Waiting to keep the appointment she made
> Meeting a man from the motor trade.

So, agreed, the world's in a mess, it needs saving. Even at home we lead separate, lonely lives. The way out of the mess is to find somebody to love. They may have dreary connections (don't we all) – say in the motor trade – but get together and within yourselves you can hack out an area where you can live liveable lives. As 'Getting Better' puts it:

> I have to admit it's getting better
> It's getting better since you've been mine.
> Me used to be a angry young man

Me hiding me head in the sand
You gave me the word
I finally heard
I'm doing the best that I can.

Most people would agree with that. If all life was about was making profits for the people you work for all week, then any sane person would go crazy. It's personal relationships and the happiness and the refuge they provide that hold a lot of people together and stop them blowing their brains out. Without somebody to love, what'd be the point of it all?

One of the exciting things about the novels of E.M.Forster is the way he probes beyond this idea, one of the central beliefs in our society. He sets it up, tests it, sees how far it stands up and works and sees where it begins to break down and fall apart.

In a talk broadcast in 1946, Forster noted that 'my books emphasise the importance of personal relationships and the private life, for I believe in them.' This belief evolved and changed, however, reshaped by Forster's own experiences. At first personal relationships are presented in his novels as the thing that makes life worth living. They're the way we escape from a society gone dismal and absurd. But in his later work this view is revised and those relationships, though still prized, are seen not as a refuge from social pressures but rather as the first victims of such pressures. Part of the way we realise that society has become vicious and needs changing is the way that it again and again aborts the efforts of people to relate normally and lovingly to one another. You can't get out of society and hide in personal relationships because those relationships are seen as precisely the point where we feel social controls and distortions at their sharpest.

But Forster was a long way from this discovery in his first novels. In them, the belief that we can somehow hide within ourselves and with our friends has no limits. Philip

22

Herriton, the hero of *Where Angels Fear to Tread* (1905) insists: 'Society *is* invincible – to a certain degree. But your real life is your own and nothing can touch it.' *A Room with a View* (1908) builds this notion right into its title. English society is mad. Lucy Honeychurch, the heroine, gets out of it by meeting not a man from the motor trade but a socialist, George Emerson. They elope to Italy and there they throw away middle-class inhibitions and blinkers and honeymoon in a room with a view – a view across the city of Florence, a view of life and its fullest possibilities.

In both of these novels and also in a third, *Arctic Summer*, which Forster began in 1911 but never finished, it's Italy that's the key. There, out in the sun and away from the dull suffocations of English Puritanism, people dare to come alive, dare to relate passionately to one another instead of just sniffing warily at each other. Two problems here. First, if personal relationships are to carry the weight that Forster wants them to, he has to show them working in an English setting. And second, more practically, after 1922 it became difficult even for liberals to have illusions about the uniquely liberating nature of Italian sun and air with Mussolini installed in power.

As early as 1910 Forster tried to show personal relationships triumphing against an English setting. The novel's called *Howards End* and it's full of a sense of menace and submerged violence. 'Life's going to be melted down, all over the world, concludes one of the characters. Against this prospect, personal relationships are placed as a refuge in the shape of a marriage between the liberal Margaret Schlegel and the conservative Henry Wilcox. But it doesn't convince. Both are empty shells by the end. Margaret has dumped her earlier radicalism and hasn't replaced it with anything. Henry is a broken-down businessman wearily arranging his will.

Then in 1913 at the age of 34 Forster's world changed. He realised that he was a homosexual. In that year he had made several visits to Edward Carpenter's communal farm near Sheffield. Carpenter was part mystic, part socialist, part sexual revolutionary. In 1896 the Labour Press had published his *Love's Coming of Age* which included a veiled defence of homosexuality as well as an examination of the sexual exploitation of women. There's a good brief account of his life and work in Sheila Rowbotham's *Hidden from History*.

Anyway, on his second or third visit to Carpenter's farm Forster's homosexuality, suppressed till then, emerged. He wrote:

> he (Carpenter) and his comrade George Merrill combined to make a profound impression on me and to touch a creative spring. George Merrill also touched my backside - gently and just above the buttocks. I believe he touched most people's. The sensation was unusual and I still remember it, as I remember the position of a long vanished tooth. It was as much psychological as physical. It seemed to go straight through the small of my back into my ideas, without involving my thoughts.
>
> 'Terminal note', *Maurice*, London 1971, p.235.

Forster's dim, deep sense of frustration, which is there in *Howards End* and which blocked his attempts to finish new novels like *Arctic Summer* and *A Passage to India*, evaporated at once. He wrote the first draft of a new novel, *Maurice*, in three months.

In its final version the novel presents us with Maurice Hall and takes him through his awful, sexually repressive public school to Cambridge. There he has a mild affair with Clive Durham, a fellow student. Clive, as he puts it, becomes normal later, gets married and runs for Parliament as a Tory. Alone and depressed, Maurice goes to his doctor and then a psychiatrist, looking for a cure. But his depression vanishes in a riotously physical relationship with Alec Scudder, a gamekeeper on Clive Durham's estate. The novel ends with Maurice and Alec determined to live together, in spite of the enormous class difference between them, in spite of the world's disapproval. Forster comments in his 'Terminal note' to the book:

> A happy ending was imperative. I shouldn't have bothered to write otherwise. I was determined that in fiction anyway two men should fall in love and remain in it for the ever and ever that fiction allows, and in this sense Maurice and Alec still roam the greenwood.... If it ended unhappily, with a lad dangling from a noose or with a suicide pact, all would be well, for there is no pornography or seduction of minors. But the lovers get away unpunished and consequently recommend crime.... the only penalty society exacts is an exile they gladly embrace.

To 'roam the greenwood' is, of course, not on as a possibility in twentieth century Britain outside the fantasy world of adverts for lavatory paper, and the unconvincingness of the phrase points to the book's weakness. If Maurice and Alec had set up in a flat together in 1913, the landlady would have been round to the police five minutes after she'd found out what they were up to and that would have been that. *Maurice* then is not so much a novel about the real world as a necessary psychological release for Forster.

At this point, at the very moment when he begins to know himself properly, Forster's career as a novelist more or less stops. *Maurice*, he felt, couldn't possibly be published 'until my death and England's.' Forster died in 1970 and *Maurice* came out in 1971. Between 1913 and 1970 he published only one novel, *A Passage to India* in 1924, and that, as we've seen, was started in 1912. In 1964 he wrote sadly in his diary: 'I should have been a more famous writer if I had written or rather published more, but sex has prevented the latter.' Forster, in short, joins a whole series of great writers of his era – men like Hardy, Wilde, Shaw, Joyce and D.H.Lawrence – whose experience shows the hollowness of pieties about British free speech. Each in different ways collided with the fact that you are free to say anything you like as long as it upsets nobody important. Say much more and they'll try to shut you up.

As a homosexual, Forster was clearly forced to re-examine his attitude towards personal relationships. A naturally shy man, he says little about this directly. But the fact is that in his early novels Forster presents personal relationships as a hideout from an oppressive society; the later, homosexual Forster realised that relationships are the first target of such a society. Relationships with other people are, after all, the way we experience society, the way we live in it and have contact with it, and it is of course on the homosexual relationship that social pressures bear heaviest, in the shape of moral disgust, empty-headed jokes, explosive disapproval, active discrimination and so on. A homosexual is forced to see that relationships are not a way out of a mad world but are instead the links that bind us into the values and tensions of that world.

Armed with this radical realisation, Forster was able to complete *A Passage to India* and able to make it a great novel. It's set in India where he spent several months and one of its major themes is the frustrated efforts of Aziz, an Indian doctor, and Fielding, an English teacher, to build a friendship. Both are men of sensitivity and goodwill but again and again their attempts to relate to each other are fractured by the stresses in Indian society, split as it is by imperialism, class, caste, religion and so on. Forster's ability to move from a grasp of an entire social structure to an investigation of what that structure means down at the personal, one-to-one level is nowhere better seen than in the famous last paragraphs of the novel. Aziz shouts at Fielding as the pair are out riding:

'Down with the English anyhow. That's certain. Clear out, you fellows, double quick, I say. We may hate one another, but we hate you most. If I don't make you go, Ahmed will, Karim will, if it's fifty five-hundred years we shall get rid of you, yes, we shall drive every blasted Englishman into the sea, and then' – he rode against him furiously – 'and then,' he concluded, half kissing him, 'you and I shall be friends.'

'Why can't we be friends now?' said the other, holding him affectionately. 'It's what I want. It's what you want.'

But the horses didn't want it – they swerved apart; the earth didn't want it, sending up rocks through which riders must pass single file; the temples, the tank, the jail, the palace, the birds, the carrion, the Guest House, that came into view as they issued from the gap and saw Mau beneath: they didn't want it, they said in their hundred voices, 'No, not yet,' and the sky said, 'No, not there.'

Individuals may want it, but what use is that when there are temples, tanks, jails, palaces and a thousand and one other moral or social or concrete barriers in the way? Break those down and then perhaps personal relationships between and within the sexes can grow and expand in ways that now we can scarcely imagine.

The young Forster had dreamed of escaping bourgeois values by finding a partner and fleeing together to a room with a view. The mature Forster realised that first you have to fight bourgeois society to build your room before you can go and live in it. But he never took the next, political step that this insight calls for. Instead he slid into the comforts that a private income and an Honorary Fellowship at King's College, Cambridge, offered. In 1953 he was made a Companion of Honour. In the 1960s when it was suggested that it was time King's College began to share its advantages a little by admitting a few extra students, he opposed the idea, telling *The Sunday Times*: 'Whereas in business generally expansion may be beneficial, it is harmful to our business, which is to produce civilised people.'

In a snotty statement like that the easy retreat from liberalism into self-defensive privilege is obviously complete, and really civilised people can have little but contempt for the attitudes and position of the old Forster. But nonetheless *A Passage to India* is still there, and it remains one of the best records of the mess capitalism makes of our relationships.

4. SEX, THE MILKMAN AND LENIN

'The book deals,' said the Attorney-General, 'with what everybody will recognize as an unsavoury subject – gratification of sexual appetite.'

Daily Sketch, quoted in Michael Bateman (ed.)
This England, Penguin 1969, p.29.

E.M. Forster died in 1970 and two years later a selection of his work called *The Life to Come and Other Stories* was published. One of the stories is called 'What Does it Matter?' and the title points to the idea that runs through the whole book. This is Forster's picture of official life in Britain, from the church through the schools, the magistrates, the police right down to your local doctor, all lined up in rows saying 'No!' Behind them people are furtively and cheerfully saying 'What does it matter?' and snatching sexual pleasure together in spite of that massive 'No!'

Take, for example, the longest story in the book called 'The Other Boat'. In this Lionel March, an Army officer, breaks away from his education in sexual frigidity and finds in a homosexual affair what Forster calls 'luxury, gaiety, kindness, unusualness and delicacy that did not exclude brutal pleasure'. To arrive at this Lionel has to grow beyond his lopsided upbringing. He remembers:

he hadn't been so much bothered by sex as were some of them. He hadn't had the time, what with his soldiering duties and his obligations at home as eldest son; and the doc said an occasional wet dream was nothing to worry about. Don't sleep on your back, though. On this simple routine he had proceeded since puberty.

op cit, London 1972, pp.192–3.

This simple routine is of course the dismal equipment with which generations of people in this country were supplied to meet the splendour of their own sexuality.

Obviously, sex is an essential human instinct – without it the species would die. But as soon as you start to talk about it and about the forms it takes you move away from the universal towards the specific, the social. In other words, when you start to talk about sexual practices and beliefs in, say, Britain, you bump up against the central fact of British life, namely class divisions.

There's a good instance of this in Forster's diary. He wrote that what he wanted was 'to love a strong young man of the lower classes, and be loved by him, and even hurt by him. That's my ticket.' On the face of it this is perhaps a surprising statement to come from a quiet Cambridge don with a large private income. Yet if we look at his fiction we find that he almost never shows people finding sexual happiness within their own circle. Again and again characters have to reach out far beyond their British middle-class setting to find a partner.

In *Maurice*, as we've already seen, the lovers are a Cambridge graduate and a gamekeeper. The same sort of pattern repeats itself in many of the short stories in the *Life to Come* collection. In 'Doctor Woolacott' it's a squire and a farmhand. In 'The Obelisk' it's a suburban housewife and a sailor. In 'The Life to Come' it's a vicar and an African chief. In 'Arthur Snatchfold' it's Sir Richard Conway and the milkman. In 'The Other Boat', it's Lionel March and a character his brother officers, with customary sensitivity, describe as 'a wog'.

You might be tempted to write all this off as one of Forster's quirks, part of the price he had to pay for all the disadvantages of a British ruling class upbringing. But once you start looking around at other writers you find that the set-up repeats itself too frequently to have anything to do with Forster's personality. Fantasising about an escape from the drawing room and Conservative Party fetes into the brutal, sweaty arms of foreigners and/or the working classes fills the fiction that the middle classes have consumed for a century and more.

Victorian pornography, for example, was aimed exclusively at the well-to-do and is full of dreams of this sort. Open Henry Spencer Ashbee's *Index of Forbidden Books* at random and instances of this are everywhere. Here's how he summarises the plot of a typical piece called *Eveline: or, The Amours and Adventures of a Lady of Fashion* published in London around 1840:

> Eveline, or Evelina, a young lady of good family, daughter of Sir John C——, allows herself to be deflowered by her father's valet on board the packet while crossing to France. She afterwards passes into the arms of her different pages, one a negro, into those of her father's coachman, with whom she knows her mother to be intimate, of her own brother and father, both of whom she, as it were, seduces. She assumes male attire, and parades the streets of Paris by night in search of adventures; grants her favours to a shoemaker, to a whole bevy of coachmen, etc.; and she fights a duel. On principle, she never allows any man of birth to enjoy her.

The association of sex and abroad is the basis of the appeal of E.M.Hull's novel *The Sheik*, a bestseller that came out in 1919. When it was filmed it gave Rudolf Valentino his most famous part. Diana Mayo the British heroine is kidnapped by Sheik Ahmed Ben Hassan, taken off to his harem and raped more or less nightly. In the end, though, she Falls In Love with him, so that makes it alright. As *Vogue* once insisted:

> There are few *Vogue* readers who have never harboured a slinking desire to be thrown across the saddle of a plunging white stallion, galloped to a palmy oasis and stuffed with dates in a striped silk prison by swarthy warriors.
>
> Quoted in *This England*, p.117.

Quite, madam.

The same sort of dream is also there in two things D.H.Lawrence wrote in 1926, the year of the General

Strike. The difference is that Lawrence is aware as the editors of *Vogue* are not that the dream is connected to the emotional emptiness of the British ruling classes and he writes out of that sense. In *The Virgin and the Gipsy*, the virgin Yvette is hard and restless in her rectory home of crossword puzzles, Horlicks and degenerated comfort. She's warmed into life by a gipsy with the 'curious dark, suave purity of all his body . . . purity like a living sneer.'

In the other work, *The First Lady Chatterley* (the first draft of *Lady Chatterley's Lover*), Lady Constance's husband Sir Clifford is paralysed below the waist from a war wound. Lawrence intends this to stand for the sexual paralysis of a whole class. Lady Constance runs from this frigidity into the bed of the gamekeeper, Parkin. By the end of the novel Parkin has left the Chatterleys to become a factory worker and secretary of the 'Communist league' in Sheffield. Constance decides to follow him there because

> there came a breath of fresh air with him, and a breath of fresh life. My lady's fucker, as he called himself so savagely! How he had hated her for not taking him full seriously in his manly fucking! Ah well! The future was still to hand!
>
> *op cit*, Penguin 1973, p.253.

Enough examples. From Victorian pornography up through *Vogue* and Valentino to the art of Forster and Lawrence, the message seems to be the same. It concerns the British middle classes, whose views can be summarised as follows. 'We in the middle classes have managed to get the sex thing in its place and under control, thank God. Sex, anyway, is basically unBritish – an unsavoury subject, as the Attorney-General once noted. Of course, there's a lot of it goes on amongst foreigners, who can't be expected to know any better, and amongst the working classes – but they're sub-human and therefore scarcely British anyway. These people have beastly thoughts and do beastly things and so breed like rabbits, as Sir Keith Joseph has proved. Give them half a chance and they're all at it –

whilst we attend to the nation's business. If we didn't it's a well known fact that the country would pretty soon go to the dogs.'

The problem is that the sex thing does rear its ugly head from time to time, so that when the British middle classes want to have a quiet think about it they are straightaway forced out of their board rooms and bored rooms. Perhaps by the Mediterranean, in a gamekeeper's hut, at the harem, in Paris, there's a milkman, a sheik, a sailor, a gipsy who can supply what's missing from their own hysterical, comfortable, empty lives? Maybe down behind a factory in Sheffield or over there, under the palm trees, people are making love unafraid, without their fathers and Our Father standing behind them with a Bible and a big stick, without Mrs Whitehouse getting ready to throw a bucket of water? There's no hope of thrills on the 8.43 into Waterloo because most of them read the *Daily Telegraph* and vote Tory, but maybe next summer in Majorca . . .? Or, to use the terms of *1984*, we in the middle classes are all paid-up members of the Anti-Sex league, but we're aware that down amongst the proles the dirty, fascinating little secret still survives.

Knockabout aside, I think there is a real significance in all this. It points to a dim sense, smothered deep in bourgeois hearts, that they don't live in the best of all possible worlds; that the society they sing the National Anthem about and praise at Rotary Club lunches is in important ways twisted and inhuman; that somewhere else, in a caravan or beyond Calais, people could and do live finer, gentler, happier, sexier lives. We mustn't laugh at these damp and unpatriotic little dreams. The fact that they exist at all is a tribute to the power of human sensuality to survive generations of Christianity and public schools.

Perhaps, you may say, all this is out of date. We now live, it says here in the newspaper, in a permissive society. Apparently this means that *Naughty Nights in a Nunnery* is being held over for another week at your local Odeon and tomorrow the *Mirror* will show you a naked nipple. What all that has to do with human freedom is obscure, though it is true that they couldn't have got away with it twenty years ago. But it's more accurate to see part of its source in the changing needs of capitalism, constantly and feverishly revolutionising itself in order to survive, though an equally important part lies in other factors like the development of reliable methods of birth control, a generation of post-war prosperity and so on.

Capitalism must go on expanding and finding fresh markets or else it begins to collapse in on itself and die. In the past this drove it to colonise and exploit Asia, Africa, the world. That business complete, it hunts for new areas to seize, turn into a product and re-sell and it's come up with sex. ('Okay, they buy plenty of Coca Cola in Kuwait now, but maybe they'll buy breasts in Burnley? We can't sell any more Weetabix in West Africa, the market's flooded, but maybe they'll pay a lot for nudes in Nebraska?')

Sections of the ruling class led by Lord Longford are upset about this shift and protest, but other sections are making far too much money out of it for their protests to be taken very seriously. Socialists, of course, take no sides in this squabble. We reject both the traditions of middle-class puritanism on the one hand and the plastic pseudo-sex of *Men Only* on the other. The former was and remains repressive, the latter is a straightforward rip-off.

What socialists offer instead is perhaps less clear, though there have been attempts to suggest what a genuinely liberated sexuality might mean. One of the best and briefest indications of this is in a letter dated 17 January 1915, that Lenin wrote to Inessa Armand. He comments on her plans for a pamphlet for working-class women as follows:

Dear Friend,

I very much advise you to write the plan of the pamphlet in as much detail as possible. Otherwise too much is unclear.

One opinion I must express here and now:

I advise you to throw out altogether number 3 – the 'demand (women's) for freedom of love'.

That is not really a proletarian but a bourgeois demand.

After all, what do you understand by that phrase? What *can* be understood by it?

1. Freedom *from* material (financial) calculations in affairs of love?

2. The same, *from* material worries?

3. From religious prejudices?

4. From prohibitions by Papa, etc.?

5. From the prejudices of 'society'?

6. From the narrow circumstances of one's environment (peasant or petty-bourgeois or bourgeois intellectual)?

7. From the fetters of the law, the courts and the police?

8. From the serious element in love?

9. From child-birth?

10. Freedom of adultery? Etc.

I have enumerated many shades (not all, of course). You have in mind, of course, not Nos. 8–10, but either Nos. 1–7 or something *similar* to Nos. 1–7.

But then for Nos. 1–7 you must choose a different wording, because freedom of love does not express this idea exactly.

And the public, the readers of the pamphlet, will *inevitably* understand by 'freedom of love', in general, something like Nos. 8–10, even *without your wishing it*.

Just because in modern society the most talkative, noisy and 'top-prominent' classes understand by 'freedom of love' Nos. 8–10, just for that very reason this is not a proletarian but a bourgeois demand.

For the proletariat Nos. 1–2 are the most important, and then Nos. 1–7, and those, in face, are not 'freedom of love'.

The thing is not what you *subjectively* 'mean' by this. The thing is the *objective logic* of class relations in affairs of love.

Friendly shake hands!
V.I.

Lenin, *On Literature and Art*, Moscow 1967, pp.196–7.

The letter is brief and therefore, as Lenin admits, leaves many questions untouched. Moreover, what were progressive demands for working class women in Czarist Russia arguably fall short of the full needs of men and women here and now. But one way of arriving at a correct sense of those needs might be to take Lenin's letter step by step, see what it still has to offer and see where its demands need changing.

5. CAPITALISM, RACISM AND JOSEPH CONRAD

In the first dozen years of the twentieth century British capitalism was in crisis. It wasn't one of the monthly joke crises invented by the newspapers whose aim is to convince any worker with an ounce of guts and patriotism to Stand Up To The Militants and forego a wage rise for the next 83 years in the national interest. No, this time it was serious. True, it didn't get in the way of the real business of life, so that historian Eric Hobsbawm has rightly called the period an 'orgy of conspicuous waste,' the great age of Biarritz, of Monte Carlo, of the country house weekend. But it did mean threats to and cuts in the standard of living of most people in this country, and that in its turn fuelled all sorts of struggles.

The roots of the crisis are outside the scope of this book, but a few examples of the way it showed itself are worth mentioning. First, inflation. The pound of 1895 was worth only 70p by 1914. That may seem scarcely any inflation at all in the light of our present experience, but coming as it did after a whole generation in which prices had steadily fallen it represented an enormous change, a change not compensated for by a matching increase in wages for the majority of people.

Then there were strikes – workers spent nearly four times as many days on strike on the eve of the First World War as they had done at the turn of the century. 1911 brought a national dock strike as well as the first national rail strike. Miners were particularly militant. Winston

Churchill tried to settle them in Tonypandy in 1911. Troops arrived and shot seven pickets, with the result that in 1912 there was the first national coal strike in British history. Union membership, 1.5 million in 1890, was up to nearly 4 million by 1914.

Ireland next. The nationalist movement was recovering from various setbacks in the 1890s and building towards the Easter Rising of 1916. The Liberal Government's attempt to grant home rule in 1912 was blocked by the House of Lords. This meant a two year delay before the bill could be enacted. The Tories took the hint and, with their customary respect for law and order and hatred of violence, began openly arming and preparing for civil war. In March 1914 they were cheered by the news that British Army officers at the Curragh Camp had refused to obey orders to mobilise against them. (When other ranks do this sort of thing it's called a mutiny and is very bad. When officers did it, it was called a crisis of conscience and was very understandable, so no one was punished.)

And then there were the women, fed up after generations on their knees and at last rising to their feet. The Women's Social and Political Union was founded in 1903 at a meeting in Mrs Pankhurst's drawing room. By 1908 they could draw half a million people to a rally in Hyde Park.

So there, briefly, crudely, was the situation. Inflation, national coal strikes, growth in working class militancy, Ireland in turmoil, women struggling for their rights, the Tories openly flirting with armed vigilante groups. Sounds familiar.

If the situation was familiar, so too was at least one of the solutions the ruling class was prepared to try. That solution was racism, the old divide and rule tactic. Keep the lower orders busy kicking each other and they'll be in no position to unite and fight their real enemies.

The victims of this racism were largely Russian and Polish Jews fleeing pogroms and discriminatory laws following the assassination of the Czar by Polish students in 1881. Estimates of the number coming to this country varied from 82,000 (the official Government figure) to 800,000 (the total put about by Tory alarmists). As early as 1886 the Earl of Dunraven and Lord Brabazon had founded the Society for the Suppression of the Immigration of Destitute Aliens. Nobody took much notice and the society faded away. Undeterred, the deeply disgusting *Evening News* tried it on again in 1891: an article on May 20 was headlined 'The Jewish Invasion' and next day it led with 'Jews as Anarchists'.[1]

Trouble was clearly brewing so mobs of ruling class hooligans started congregating, looking for a chance to put the boot in. The Earl of Dunraven now founded the Association for the Prevention of the Immigration of Destitute Aliens (APIDA). His vice-presidents included the Dukes of Abercorn and of Montrose, the Earl of Egmont, Earl Ferrers, Lady Sandhurst, Lady Dorothy Nevill plus the odd bishop and vicar. Lord Charles Beresford thundered that the immigrants were an 'incubator for Communism and Socialism'. The Hon. William Le Poer Trench, a member of APIDA, ran for Parliament in Whitechapel but got thrashed.

However, the hooligans plugged away and in 1905 got the Tory Government under Balfour to pass the Aliens Act. This act made entry much more difficult, introduced the term 'undesirable alien' into the English language and gave the Home Secretary much wider powers to throw out people already here. It also made poverty a crime – an immigrant could be expelled for 'living under insanitary conditions due to overcrowding'.

Literature shared in these issues. In 1906 Robert Tressell started to write his socialist classic, *The Ragged Trousered Philanthropists*, and devoted the very first chapter to contesting various racist arguments, evidence of the seriousness with which he viewed them as a threat to working-class unity and organisation. On the other hand, a standard chunk of racism and bestselling novel of the period was Guy Thorne's *When It Was Dark*, first published in 1903. The villain of this piece is a Jewish millionaire, Constantine Schuabe, who plots to overthrow Christian civilisation by faking archaeological evidence to disprove the story of Christ's resurrection. The fraud is believed for a while so things fall apart and the number of rapes doubles. Fortunately a plucky curate called Basil and Gertrude, a whore with a heart of gold, unmask the rogue and the Stock Exchange recovers in a twinkling.[2]

Which brings us to Joseph Conrad. In 1905, the Government was busy as we've already seen acquiring powers to expel Russian and Polish immigrants for the crime of poverty. Yet the same year Balfour, the Tory Prime Minister, arranged for Conrad, an impoverished novelist of Polish origin, to receive a grant of £500 'in view of the quality of his work and his need for money'. Why? Why didn't Balfour try to throw him out like the rest? To answer that we need to look briefly at the man and the work whose quality so pleased the Prime Minister.

In 1857 Conrad had been born Jozef Teodor Konrad Korzeniowski of Polish parents living in the Ukraine. They died when he was a boy and at the age of 16 he took up a career as a merchant sailor. He first served on an English ship at the age of 20. By the time he was 29 he had become a naturalized British subject and had earned a Board of Trade master's certificate. His views at this time were fairly typical of an officer in the Merchant Service: brisk, elitist and right wing. Thus in 1885 we find him writing a couple of letters to a friend. The first thanks him for sending a copy of the *Daily Telegraph*, and the second has this to say about contemporary politics:

the International Socialist Association are triumphant, and every disreputable ragamuffin in Europe feels that the day of universal brotherhood, despoliation and disorder is coming apace, and nurses day-dreams of well-plenished pockets amongst the ruin of all that is respectable, venerable and holy. The great British Empire went over the edge, and yet on to the inclined plane of social progress and radical reform. The downward movement is hardly perceptible yet, and the clever men who start it may flatter themselves with the progress; but they will soon find that the fate of the nation is out of their hands now! The Alpine avalanche rolls quicker and quicker as it nears the abyss – its ultimate destination! Where's the man to stop the crashing avalanche?

Where's the man to stop the rush of social-democratic ideas? The opportunity and the day have come and are gone! Believe me: gone for ever! For the sun is set and the last barrier removed. England was the only barrier to the pressure of infernal doctrines born in continental back-slums. Now, there is nothing!

Quoted in Jocelyn Baines,
Joseph Conrad, London 1960, pp.80-81.

Sadly, Conrad never really passed beyond the blinkered world of *Daily Telegraph* politics. When he retired from the sea ten years later in order to write, it was the same set of thin, reactionary ideas that he began to shape into fictional forms.

In October 1906, a year after the passage of the Aliens Act, Conrad's novel *The Secret Agent: A Simple Tale* began to appear in serial form. F. R. Leavis, who's probably the best known English literary critic, uses the following phrases to describe it in his book *The Great Tradition:* 'indubitably a classic and a masterpiece . . . classical in its maturity of attitude . . . sophisticated moral interest . . . one of the most astonishing triumphs of genius in fiction . . . one of Conrad's two supreme masterpieces, one of the two unquestionable classics of the first order that he added to the English novel . . . subtle and triumphant complexity of its art' and so on.

F. R. Leavis notwithstanding, the fact that *The Secret Agent* was serialised in a U.S. magazine called *Ridgeway's: a Militant Weekly for God and Country* is an accurate give-away, and it really is difficult to take the book much more seriously than the other piece of rubbish, Guy Thorne's *When It Was Dark*, that we mentioned earlier. The main character, Adolf Verloc, runs a porn shop in Soho with his wife Winnie. In his spare time he's an agent provocateur hired by the Czarist Russian Embassy to move in various anarchist and revolutionary groups. He also does a bit of spying on behalf of the British police.

The climax comes after he inadvertently blows up Winnie's brother during one of his murky escapades. Appalled, Winnie murders Verloc with the carving knife and rushes out of the shop into the arms of Comrade Ossipon, one of Verloc's contacts. She hands over to him all of Verloc's savings and together they decide to flit to St. Malo. However, clever Comrade Ossipon slips off the train with Verloc's money just as it pulls out of the station, leaving abandoned Winnie to jump off the cross-Channel ferry in despairing suicide.

The point of the story is on the one hand straight-forward flattery of the fuzz who have the thankless task of dealing with these people – the Russian ambassador at the end is 'almost awed by the miraculous cleverness of the English police'. On the other hand it's an attempt to present all revolutionaries as a poisonous gaggle of drunks, bores, foreigners, maniacs, drones, fatties, loons, and physical and racial degenerates. Read for example the description of Comrade Ossipon and you reach straight back both to the nasty racism and Tory hysteria behind the 1905 Aliens Act and to the sort of quality in Conrad that Balfour had earlier thought worth £500: 'A bush of crinkly yellow hair topped his red, freckled face, with a flattened nose and prominent mouth cast in the rough mould of the negro type. His almond-shaped eyes leered languidly over the high cheek-bones.'

The whole is peppered with asides that point to a political grasp roughly on a par with that of Lord Charles Beresford and Guy Thorne. Conrad assures us knowingly that: 'The majority of revolutionists are the enemies of discipline and fatigue mostly The majority of revolutionists at that time called themselves Bolsheviks, at least in the Russian context Conrad is describing. Indeed, as *The Secret Agent* was being printed in London in the summer of 1907 Bolsheviks such as Lenin and Djugashvili-Ivanovich (later known as Stalin) were also in London, attending the fifth congress of the Russian Social Democratic Party. Even someone as politically naive as, say, the editor of the *Daily Telegraph* would probably hesitate to call people like Stalin an 'enemy of discipline'.

And so on. The standard revolutionary is not bothered about the Czar's police, exploitation, starvation and the rest, he's just 'an insolent and venomous evoker of sinister impulses which lurk in the blind envy and exasperated vanity of ignorance' – the overripe, rotten language here matches the overripe, rotten idea. The readers of *Ridgeway's: a Militant Weekly for God and Country* may have lapped it up, but F. R. Leavis is a big boy now and he ought to be a little more discriminating.

Conrad's next novel, *Under Western Eyes*, was also a study of Russian revolutionaries, this time operating in St Petersburg and in exile in Geneva. It's worth a look because it's a good example of an enormous contradiction that's still widely believed in. Thesis number one is that all human beings are the same – this because of their common, unchanging human nature. It is for this reason that all attempts at change, especially revolutionary change, are a waste of time, as the novel demonstrates. Conrad insists as much in an Author's Note he added to the 1920 edition; he wonders at the revolutionaries'

strange conviction that a fundamental change of hearts must follow the downfall of any given human institutions. These people are unable to see that all they can effect is merely a change of names. The oppressors and the oppressed are all Russians together; and the world is brought once more face to face with the truth of the saying that the tiger cannot change his stripes nor the leopard his spots.

Thesis number two is that human beings are unimaginably different – split into utterly contrasting racial groups. Hence the novel suggests that it's almost impossibly difficult for British readers to understand some of the things the Russians get up to. Indeed, as the English teacher who narrates the story points out again and again, he can scarcely understand them himself. We can only come near it if we remember we're far from the Home Counties and make huge allowances for the characters and their thoughts:

> If to the Western reader they appear shocking, inappropriate, or even improper, it must be remembered that as to the first this may be the effect of my crude statement. For the rest I will only remark here that this is not a story of the West of Europe.
>
> *Under Western Eyes*, Penguin 1957, p.28.

Small problem. Thesis number one (all human beings are the same) contradicts thesis number two (all human beings are different). Contradicts it to an extent that makes the novel more or less worthless. Either we all belong to such totally different racial groups that the habits and deficiencies of Russian revolutionaries have no relevance to the British situation, which destroys the novel's purpose. Or we're all the same and those habits and deficiencies *are* relevant – in which case the novel's frequent insistence on total difference is muddled eyewash. But then anyone who's listened to Enoch Powell knows that muddled eyewash lies at the centre of all racist theory.

---

[1] Details in this and the following paragraph from Bernard Gainer, *The Alien Invasion: the Origins of the Aliens Act of 1905*, London 1972.

[2] There's a great knockabout account of this dreadful book in Claud Cockburn's *Bestseller: the Books that Everyone Reads, 1900–1939*, London 1972.

6. THE SINKING OF THE TITANIC: IS BRITAIN GOING UNDER ALONG WITH IT?

Put this book down for five minutes if you can bear to and switch on the TV. The odds are that if there's a current affairs programme on there'll be a man in a hundred guinea suit and a haircut, from *The Economist*, say, or the *New Statesman* or the C B I, assuring you that the way things are going with the energy crisis, inflation, lack of real leadership at the top and so on, democracy, nay western civilisation as we have known it, is quite possibly doomed in our time for this generation and we shall not look on its like again. Or some such drivel. Profound pessimism seems as fashionable at the moment as existentialism a generation ago. It's a dreary philosophy but since it's so widespread we'd better take a look at it.

One way of doing that is to turn to the novels and poems of a man who's been described as the greatest English pessimist, Thomas Hardy. His books express that philosophy intensely and fully, and by looking at some of them we can trace its roots, appeal and limitations.

Hardy was born at Bockhampton, Dorset, in 1840. His father was a small builder employing half-a-dozen men but his family on his mother's side were extremely poor. 1840 was a bad time to be born in Dorset. Average farm wages at less than 40p a week were the lowest of any county in England – 40p a week when it cost the labourers 5p a loaf to buy back the bread they made for their masters.

When times are bad there are two things you can do about it: you can try revolution and you can try reforms.

Both appeared to have been tried in Dorset in the ten years before Hardy's birth, and both appeared to have failed. In 1830 there had been the Captain Swing revolts right across the southern counties, a spontaneous eruption of demonstrations, rick burning and machine smashing. This bitter but politically naive protest against high unemployment and low wages met with fierce repression. At Tisbury, 25 miles from Hardy's birthplace, John Hardy, a farm labourer and just possibly a distant relative, was first to die, shot down by a troop of yeomanry. By the end of 1832, the revolt was smashed. Nearly 2,000 had been arrested. Of these, 19 were executed, 644 sent to prison and 505 transported to Australia and Tasmania. A generation of militants was effectively silenced.

But the people wouldn't lie down. In 1834, rebellion having failed, they tried reform. At Tolpuddle, six miles from Hardy's birthplace, farm labourers set about forming a trade union. Again, the same sensitive, enlightened and sympathetic response from the ruling class: arrest and transportation.

So it was into the aftermath of these two terrible defeats for the people of Dorset that Hardy was born in 1840. What he seems to have found around him is a sort of gloomy stoicism, a feeling that life would never be much good, that there was nothing you could do about it, so you'd best grin and bear it. As a child he practised copperplate handwriting and his copybooks still survive. 'Passion is a bad counsellor'; 'Quit vicious habits'; 'Encourage diligence', he was told to write – standard Victorian morals perhaps, but ones that also speak of the dull resignation of mid-nineteenth century Dorset.

Even at the age of thirty we find him recording in a notebook: 'Mother's notion (and also mine) – that a figure stands in our van with arm uplifted to knock us back from any pleasant prospect we indulge in as probable.' Clearly Hardy's mother, after the appalling poverty of her youth and the broken hopes of the 1830s, had picked up like many of her class a quiet pessimism as a kind of psychological survival strategy. Don't expect much so you won't be disappointed when you don't get much. If you try for more there'll be troops to shoot you, the figure with arm uplifted to knock you back, so keep your head down, encourage diligence, quit vicious habits and maybe they'll leave you alone. This philosophy Hardy absorbed as a child and never really abandoned.

After work in an architect's office in London, Hardy at the age of 27 turned to literature and wrote a novel he called *The Poor Man and the Lady*. In his autobiography he says it was a socialist novel. He sent it to Macmillans the publishers who rejected it. A letter from Alexander Macmillan told him that the attacks it contained on middle-class heartlessness towards the working classes were intolerably overdone. Hardy then sent the book to the publishers Chapman and Hall and it was rejected again. George Meredith, who returned the manuscript, told him that he must avoid being revolutionary at the start of his career or the reviewers would annihilate him. Once again, then, Hardy was faced with the figure with arm uplifted saying 'No!', and this time he gave in. He burnt the manuscript of *The Poor Man and the Lady* and wrote instead the kind of novel that Meredith cynically urged – a book with, in Meredith's phrase, a more purely artistic purpose. The result, *Desperate Remedies*, was published in 1871 and is one of the worst novels in the English language.

In the next twenty years Hardy wrote another dozen novels, steadily building up his own following amongst the reading public. He became a saleable commodity and so publishers were prepared to accept, with certain cuts and reservations, the kind of novel he really wanted to write rather than the high-minded rubbish suggested by Meredith and enjoyed by reviewers. So it was that in 1895 he came to publish his last novel, *Jude the Obscure*.

Into the character of Jude Hardy poured all the hopes and frustations of a lifetime. Jude like Hardy is a stone-mason, a builder. Like Hardy he dreams of a university education but is 'elbowed off the pavement by the million-aires' sons.' Like Hardy his search for emotional fulfilment ends in the trap of a failed marriage. Hardy through the figure of Jude presents a whole series of human hopes – hopes for meaningful work, for a decent education, for liberated sexuality – and shows them all systematically denied by Victorian narrowness and commercialism. Jude ends defeated and dies of consumption. As he's laid out for burial, crowds outside celebrate the honorary degrees awarded to 'the Duke of Hamptonshire and a lot more illustrious gents of that sort'.

A few people – Havelock Ellis for example – liked the book and said so, and thousands bought it and were moved. But the ruling classes in general responded to this powerful protest with outrage. Bishop How of Wakefield persuaded the local library to ban the book and publicly burnt a copy – 'probably in his despair at not being able to burn me', Hardy wryly commented. In January 1896 Mrs Oliphant, writing in *Blackwood's*, a leading journal of Tory opinion, thought the book was 'disgusting' and 'coarsely indecent,' full of 'grossness, indecency and horror'.

Hardy was hurt by this. Four years earlier, after a bitter attack on him in the liberal *Saturday Review*, he had written in a notebook: 'If this sort of thing continues, no more novel-writing for me. A man must be a fool to deliberately stand up to be shot at.' In 1830 John Hardy from Wiltshire stood up in protest and was literally shot down. In 1895 Thomas Hardy from Dorset stood up in protest and was metaphorically shot down. He retired into a thirty year career as a poet, a career that began with radical hopes, hopes that he could say more in verse and get away with it, but these hopes never materialised.

We can see what happened to Hardy the poet if we

47

look at one of his best known poems. It's called 'The Convergence of the Twain: Lines on the loss of the *Titanic*' and it was first printed in the programme of a charity concert in aid of the *Titanic* Disaster Fund given at Covent Garden on May 14, 1912. Here's the poem in full. It opens with a vision of the liner, sunk after hitting an iceberg and lying on the bottom of the Atlantic:

I

In a solitude of the sea
Deep from human vanity,
And the Pride of Life that planned her, stilly couches she.

II

Steel chambers, late the pyres
Of her salamandrine fires,
Cold currents thrid, and turn to rhythmic tidal lyres.

III

Over the mirrors meant
To glass the opulent
The sea-worm crawls – grotesque, slimed, dumb, indifferent.

IV

Jewels in joy designed
To ravish the sensuous mind
Lie lightless, all their sparkles bleared and black and blind.

V

Dim moon-eyed fishes near
Gaze at the gilded gear
And query: "What does this vaingloriousness down here?"

VI

Well: while was fashioning
This creature of cleaving wing,
The Immanent Will that stirs and urges everything

VII

Prepared a sinister mate
For her – so gaily great –
A Shape of Ice, for the time far and dissociate.

VIII

And as the smart ship grew
In stature, grace and hue,
In shadowy silent distance grew the Iceberg too.

IX

Alien they seemed to be:
No mortal eye could see
The intimate welding of their later history,

X

Or sign that they were bent
By paths coincident
On being anon twin halves of one august event.

XI

Till the Spinner of the Years
Said "Now!" And each one hears,
And consummation comes, and jars two hemispheres.

We know quite a lot about the sinking of the *Titanic*. We know, for example, that 1,513 lives were lost when it went down. We know that there were lifeboats for first-class passengers only, so that while 63 per cent of them were saved, 75 per cent of the third-class passengers died.

Turn to Hardy's poem in the light of those facts and the limitations of stoic pessimism are at once clear. True, there's a vague radical unease about the vaingloriousness and opulence of it all, but in the end the fault seems to lie with the Immanent Will and the Spinner of the Years, whoever they might be. We know they had nothing to do with it. The *Titanic* sank because of commercial greed in the pursuit of the Blue Riband — the ship was travelling too fast and too far north. It sank with heavy losses because third-class lifeboats were left out to boost profits. But blame it all on the Spinner of the Years and any real analysis of the event is paralysed. Others made that analysis, learnt from it and got the laws changed. They have prevented the same sort of disaster happening again because they recognised that its origins lay in human decisions which could and must be altered. But say the Immanent Will did it and all you can do is fall on your knees and hope He (She? It?) doesn't do it again, please.

You may say in Hardy's defence that this is a 33-line poem, not a 4-volume Government report on the disaster. Okay. Sit down yourself and write a 33-line poem on, say, the Isle of Man Summerland fire in 1973 or the Flixborough factory explosion in 1974. What are you going to talk about? On the one hand, are you for example going to say anything about cost cutting on safety in the interests of higher productivity and profits? Are you going to note small details like the fact that the architects who were responsible for the use of the lethal acrylic sheeting at Summerland got off scot free at the enquiry? Are you at least going to mention that lots of people were killed and you're sad and angry about it? If you write that sort of poem you just might move some readers and you might help them towards understanding and mastering their lives and the conditions that govern them.

Or, on the other hand, are you going to slide past the very mention of dead bodies and muse instead about the disappearance of a fun palace or a factory? Are you going to blame it all on Fate or Chance and claim that 'no mortal eye could see' that this might happen? Are you going to betray the fact that you're not really looking at what went on with lots of tired verbiage about 'paths coincident', 'salamandrine fires' and 'august event'? If you write that sort of poem it stands a good chance of being printed, like Hardy's, in the programme of a charity concert organised for the victims' dependents by the people who killed them. Write lots more poems like that and, like Hardy, you too in your old age might get the Order of Merit, be offered a knighthood and have the Prince of Wales drop in for tea.

In short there's nothing a port-sodden blimp loves

more than a good old stoic pessimist. He puts his head down, takes what's coming to him and doesn't complain. If the Tories say what you need is two million unemployed or the Labour Party claims that a cut in your standard of living will do instead, then so be it, you take it bravely and encourage others to do the same. Your pessimism and stoicism mean you can do nothing else. What began, as we saw earlier, as a sort of survival strategy in 1840s Dorset in the wake of terrible defeats had become for Hardy by the twentieth century a lame belief, ruling out all action for change or self-defence.

Thomas Hardy did act on occasion, like John Hardy before him, but both were shot down because either they were politically inarticulate or because they acted alone. The way out of this bind is to act together and act politically armed. Hardy moved in that direction with his lost novel *The Poor Man and the Lady*, and moved towards it again in *Jude the Obscure* with its sense of the social, collective solutions to the problems that break individuals like Jude and his hopes for education. But in the end he backed away and in old age was left with the ironic consolations of honorary degrees from the universities of Aberdeen, Cambridge, Oxford, St.Andrew's and Bristol.

Hardy was no fool. He knew and wrote in *Jude* that capitalist society was no way for human beings to live. Great writers and great contemporaries of Hardy like William Morris and Robert Tressell came to the same conclusion. So did millions of other men and women around the world. It drove them to work for the socialist alternative. Hardy didn't take this step. Cut off from any sense of an alternative, he was left to face the future with deep pessimism. Cut off from any sense of alternatives, it's about all you've got. Switch on that TV discussion and watch the pundits snuffling gloomily over their brandies and see for yourself.

51

7. WOMEN IN THE NINETEENTH CENTURY

or

Mummy, where does literature come from?
From heaven, dear.
Now go back to sleep and don't be asking
questions.

What causes literature? The Greeks thought it was the Muses. Most teachers of English have dropped this explanation as unsatisfactory but by and large they haven't replaced it with anything else. Literature is just there and on that basis it is taught. How it comes to be there is shrouded in decent mystery. Like most decent mysteries, it's worth asking questions about if only because, as Shaw put it, 'decency is indecency's conspiracy of silence.'

Marxists claim that literature is a reflection of the real world – sometimes a crude reflection, but sometimes, especially if the literature is any good, the reflection is complex, dialectical, highly mediated. So what does that mean? We can answer that by taking an example – by looking first of all at the situation of middle-class women in the nineteenth century and then at the way this situation is re-created in the work of five authors in five different countries.

The first thing to note about that situation is that it was extremely boring. In England middle-class prosperity meant that one-sixth of the employed population were domestic servants. Hence the middle-class woman was normally freed from the drudgery of housework, but freed only into a gilded cage. Thackeray in Chapter 42 of his 1848 novel *Vanity Fair* describes Jane Osborne's 'awful existence' as she confronts her father at breakfast:

> She remained silent opposite to him, listening to the urn hissing, and sitting in tremor while the parent read his paper and consumed his accustomed portion of muffins and tea. At half-past nine he

rose and went to the City, and she was almost free till dinner-time, to make visitations in the kitchen and to scold the servants; to drive abroad and descend upon the tradesmen, who were prodigiously respectful; to leave her cards and her papa's at the great glum respectable houses of their City friends; or to sit alone in the large drawing-room, expecting visitors; and working at a huge piece of worsted by the fire, on the sofa, hard by the great Iphigenia clock, which ticked and tolled with mournful loudness in the dreary room. The great glass over the mantelpiece, faced by the other great console glass at the opposite end of the room, increased and multiplied between them the brown Holland bag in which the chandelier hung, until you saw these brown Holland bags fading away in endless perspectives, and this apartment of Miss Osborne's seemed the centre of a system of drawing-rooms.

It's all there, right down to neat little details like the Iphigenia clock – Iphigenia being the most famous example in Greek literature of woman as obedient sacrificial victim. Then there's the sense, conveyed through the image of the mirrors, of life as an infinite series of empty repetitions. From the prodigiously respectful tradesman to the whole atmosphere of nagging aimlessness, it's a perfect picture of the 'lady of civilisation' that Engels described as 'surrounded by false homage and estranged from all real work.'

If you make someone look an idiot to suit yourself you need to reassure her by pointing out that her position is quite natural. Thackeray's Jane Osborne is about as active and useful as a rubber shovel, but the experts insisted that this was biologically determined. William Acton's *The Functions and Disorders of the Reproductive Organs*, first published in 1857 and in its eighth edition on both sides of the Atlantic by 1894, may be taken as a standard medical textbook of the time. It described one aspect of women's passivity – sexual passivity – as follows:

I should say that the majority of women (happily for them) are not very much troubled with sexual feeling of any kind. . . . The best mothers, wives, and managers of households, know little or nothing of sexual indulgences. Love of home, children, and domestic duties, are the only passions they feel

53

> As a general rule, a modest woman seldom desires any sexual gratification for herself. She submits to her husband, but only to please him; and, but for the desire of maternity, would far rather be relieved from his attentions.[1]

So much for the ornamental role of the middle-class woman and the justifying ideology supplied in its wake by the experts. If we turn from this absurdity to the portrayal of women by five of the nineteenth century's most significant writers, we can see in imaginative terms some of the tensions generated by this absurdity being relived and attacked.

In the year that *Functions and Disorders of the Reproductive Organs* was first published, Flaubert was bringing out his novel *Madame Bovary* in France. In 1878 the Russian novelist Tolstoy published *Anna Karenin* at the same time as Thomas Hardy's English novel *The Return of the Native*. The American Henry James's short story *Daisy Miller* came out the next year, 1879, and the Norwegian Henrik Ibsen's play *Hedda Gabler* followed in 1890.

In all five the story is nearly the same: a spirited, far from passive middle-class heroine sets off, more or less alone, on a confused and partial revolt against her society and the confining careers and models of conduct it offers her. The result in every case is defeat and death, death which in four cases is suicide. Emma Bovary swallows rat poison, Anna Karenin jumps under a train, Hardy's Eustacia Vye drowns herself, Daisy Miller dies of malaria and Hedda Gabler blows her brains out.

Five stories so closely parallel appearing in five different places within a generation provide either a supercolossal intercontinental ballistic coincidence or evidence that literature in some way reflects the real world. The books are broadly similar because they all have the same root, and that is the authors' shared sense of the /tragic gap between women's full needs and abilities and the dwarf lives offered them by nineteenth century capitalism.

Broadly similar but not identical. The five books are

worth looking at in a little more detail because each author selects and emphasises particular angles depending on his own experiences and convictions.

Emma Bovary leads two lives. On the one hand there are the flabby romantic dreams which she, like all young girls, is fed. 'A certain agitation,' says Flaubert, using deliberately overstuffed language, 'caused by the presence of this man had sufficed to make her believe herself possessed at last of that wonderful passion which hitherto had hovered above her like a great bird of rosy plumage in the splendour of a poetic heaven.' On the other hand there's the dismal bourgeois reality of the man she marries: 'Charles's conversation was as flat as a street pavement, on which everybody's ideas trudged past in their workaday dress, provoking no emotion, no laughter, no dreams.' This contrast persists to the end, an appalling chasm between the squalid facts of bourgeois life and death and the sentimental and self-congratulatory image that that life has of itself. As Emma dies, vomiting blood, outside in the street a blind beggar sings:

> When the sun shines warm above
> It turns a maiden's thoughts to love.

The last moments of Tolstoy's Anna Karenin are full of obsessive alienation from other people. She's isolated and vulnerable, always liable to neurotic despair after a feeble revolt from her husband. At Nizhny station, men peer into her face and whisper to one another – 'something vile no doubt.' 'A mis-shapen lady' passes. Anna is 'appalled at her hideousness', at the 'grotesque and affected girl' who accompanies her and at the 'grimy, deformed-looking peasant' who follows. A husband and wife enter her carriage and she finds them 'repellent'. More men stare at her. She searches in panic for an escape because: 'Everything is false and evil – all lies and deceit!' She gets out of the carriage and hatred of humanity explodes into hatred of self: 'I shall punish him (her lover Vronsky) and escape from them all and from myself.' She steps under a goods train.

What drives Eustacia Vye in *The Return of the Native* to suicide is her sense of the impossibility of living a fulfilled life after many muddled struggles to achieve it. When a child she had wanted to be a man – her heroes were William the Conqueror, Strafford and Napoleon. As a woman she plays a man's role – she takes the part of the Turkish Knight killed by St George in a Christmas play. But when she marries she is forced to confront her economically and emotionally dependent status as wife. Moments before drowning she wavers between a wan husband and a third-rate lover:

> 'Can I go, can I go?' she moaned. 'He's not *great* enough for me to give myself to – he does not suffice for my desire! . . . If he had been a Saul or a Buonaparte – ah! But to break my marriage vow for him – it is too poor a luxury! . . . And I have no money to go alone! And if I could, what comfort to me? I must drag on next year, as I have dragged on this year, and the year after that as before. How I have tried and tried to be a splendid woman, and how destiny has been against me! . . . I do not deserve my lot!' she cried in a frenzy of bitter revolt. 'O, the cruelty of putting me into this ill-conceived world! I was capable of much; but I have been injured and blighted and crushed by things beyond my control!'

In his miniature portrait of Daisy Miller, Henry James suggests the awful punishment waiting for the woman who steps an inch out of line. Daisy, on holiday in Rome, visits the Colosseum by moonlight with a young Italian. Intolerable, as the Nonconformist conscience in the shape of Mr. Winterbourne hastens to tell her. Within a day or two she's down with the malaria he warned her she'd catch there and she's dead a week later. Serve her right, and let that be a warning to the rest of you out there to do as the man says.

What Ibsen examines through Hedda Gabler is the kind of stunted and perverse personality that could grow in the stunted and perverse situation of the nineteenth century middle-class woman. Cut off from all meaningful activity and afraid to drive towards it because of a conventional fear of causing scandal, Hedda conceives a brooding admiration for Lovborg who does challenge bourgeois conventions – an uncritical admiration for action that comes easily to a figure confined to passive observation. Like Hardy's Eustacia, Hedda, after a life of repressed fantasy, is eventually faced with the reality of her unfreedom and like Eustacia she kills herself to avoid living that reality.

Bourgeois society looked at the critical reflection of itself in its own literature and was annoyed. The *Revue de Paris* which serialised *Madame Bovary* was prosecuted for 'outrage to public morals and religion'. The Russian magazine that carried *Anna Karenin* in monthly parts rejected the final section. Ibsen was rechristened 'Ibscene' and called a 'muck-ferreting dog' by the British press. That press also attacked Hardy and was part of the reason why he gave up novel writing altogether in 1895.

Clearly bourgeois literature could pose and analyse the problem but could not solve it. Approaches to a solution could only come not from men like these authors but from women themselves. And they could only come not from literature but from life itself, from action in the day-to-day as opposed to the imaginative world.

In 1883, shortly after Eustacia Vye had felt 'crushed by things beyond my control', Engels wrote gloomily from England to Bebel in Germany: 'Do not on any account whatever let yourself be bamboozled into thinking that there is a real proletarian movement going on here.' Yet six years later he writes to Sorge: 'The movement has now got going at last and I believe for good.' The political climate changed sharply in the eighties and suddenly the boundaries of the possible seemed much wider. As Hedda Gabler the last of our five heroines shot herself in lonely desperation on the London stage, working-class women began to fight their way beyond despair. Sheila Rowbotham has described part of that fight in *Hidden from History:*

> From 1888 to around 1892 there was a considerable amount of spontaneous industrial action not only by men but also by women who had never organised before. The match-girls' strike is the best known because of the publicity the socialist Annie Besant gave it in papers and journals. However *Commonweal*, the paper of the Socialist League, reported several other incidents of female militancy in the same year. Blanket weavers in Heckmondwike, female cigarmakers in Nottingham, girls in a tin box manufactory in London, who pelted men who continued to work after they came out with red-ochre and flour, cotton workers, and jute workers in Dundee, took action spontaneously in 1888. The reasons for striking varied, from demands for increases to resistance to cuts, or opposition to fines. Again in 1899 mill girls in Kilmarnock came out over the bad quality of yarn they were being given. At Alverthorpe, near Wakefield, woollen weavers, women and girls, rejected a reduced rate and marched in procession headed by girls with concertinas. . .
>
> In London too women workers were helped by the new unionists and by socialists. Laundresses tried to make a union. They were supported by 27 trades councils and held a joint demonstration with railway workers in July 1891 in Hyde Park. According to the records of the Women's Trade Union League this was the first demonstration of working women in the Park . . .
>
> *op cit*, London 1973, pp.61-2.

Middle-class women began organising to obtain the vote at the same time. The Women's Franchise League was formed in 1889 to be followed by the Women's Social and Political Union in 1903.

A final anecdote to illustrate the immense advances of those years. In 1879 as we've already seen Henry James's fictional American heroine Daisy Miller made a tiny personal gesture of rebellion and was promptly nailed by the mosquitoes. In 1912 some of her countrywomen in Lawrence, Massachusetts, struck against pay cuts, held solid for over two months and won important concessions for a quarter of a million textile workers. During one of their demonstrations a couple of girl spinners carried a banner: 'We want bread and roses too.' This moved James Oppenheim to write his poem 'Bread and Roses' which ends:

> As we come marching, marching, unnumbered women dead
> Go crying through our singing their ancient cry for bread.
> Small art and love and beauty their drudging spirits knew.
> Yes, it is bread we fight for – but we fight for roses, too!
>
> As we come marching, marching, we bring the greater days.
> The rising of the women means the rising of the race.
> No more the drudge and idler – ten that toil where one reposes,
> But a sharing of life's glories: Bread and roses! Bread and roses![2]

---

[1] Quoted in Steven Marcus, *The Other Victorians*, New York 1967, pp.31-2.

[2] Text from Edith Fowke & Joe Glazer, *Songs of Work and Protest*, New York 1973, p.71. The five works discussed in this section are all available in paperback. *Hedda Gabler* is a Methuen's Theatre Classic and *The Return of the Native* is a Macmillan's Papermac. The other three – *Madame Bovary, Anna Karenin* and *Daisy Miller* – are Penguins. All references in this section are to these editions.

8. HANDS, KNEES AND A BOOK BY DICKENS

Remember You're a Womble!

The fact that you're reading this means that you're human and that in turn means that you've got a brain, eyes, hands, legs, sexual organs and so on. They make up the full you. It's subversive to realise how often society has tried to deny or twist or split up that fullness in its own interests. Under capitalism, for example, complex human beings developing all their capacities don't fit in at all well. The system's not designed for them or their comfort, any more than a factory bench or a typist's stool is designed for the comfort of the worker sitting on it. To fit in happily you shouldn't be a man or a woman but some sort of Womble – tame, hard working and only half human.

Literature has often recorded attempts by employers to produce a race of uncomplaining Wombles. In 1854, for instance. Dickens called Manchester Coketown and described it and its people this way in Chapter 10 of his novel *Hard Times*:

> In the hardest working part of Coketown; in the innermost fortifications of that ugly citadel, where Nature was as strongly bricked out as killing airs and gases were bricked in; at the heart of the labyrinth of narrow courts upon courts, and close streets upon streets, which had come into existence piecemeal, every piece in a violent hurry for some one man's purpose, and the whole an unnatural family, shouldering, and trampling, and pressing one another to death; in the last close nook of this great exhausted receiver, where the chimneys, for want of air to make a draught, were built in an immense variety of stunted and crooked shapes, as though every house put out a sign of the kind of people who might

be expected to be born in it; among the multitude of Coketown, generically called 'the Hands,' – a race who would have found more favour with some people, if Providence had seen fit to make them only hands, or, like the lower creatures of the seashore, only hands and stomachs – lived a certain Stephen Blackpool, forty years of age.

Stephen looked older, but he had had a hard life. It is said that every life has its roses and thorns; there seemed, however, to have been a misadventure or mistake in Stephen's case, whereby somebody else had become possessed of his roses, and he had become possessed of the same somebody else's thorns in addition to his own. He had known, to use his own words, a peck of trouble. He was usually called Old Stephen, in a kind of rough homage to the fact.

A rather stooping man, with a knitted brow, a pondering expression of face, and a hard-looking head sufficiently capacious, on which his iron-grey hair lay long and thin, Old Stephen might have passed for a particularly intelligent man in his condition. Yet he was not. He took no place among those remarkable 'Hands', who, piecing together their broken intervals of leisure through many years, had mastered difficult sciences, and acquired a knowledge of most unlikely things. He held no station among the Hands who could make speeches and carry on debates. Thousands of his compeers could talk much better than he, at any time. He was a good power-loom weaver, and a man of perfect integrity.

What bosses – or 'some people' as Dickens calls them in that first paragraph – need are Stephen's hands, the hands that work the power-loom and make a profit for the man who owns it. 'Hand', of course, was and still remains in many places the common term for a factory worker. It's how he's defined. His eyes don't matter – what use are they anyway, when all that surrounds him is the ugliness of Coketown that Dickens lays out here. Better that he shouldn't see these things – really see them for what they are. His mind doesn't matter either – it might give him ideas above his station and anyway you couldn't make money out of it in those days.

Stephen wanders through *Hard Times* in a puzzled haze, aware that something is wrong but unable to focus it, unable to find words for it so that he can begin to attack it. His catchphrase is ''Tis a muddle' – a muddle whose roots are hidden from him so that he refuses to join the union. In the end he drops absurdly to his death down a disused pitshaft. He's one of the very first industrial workers to appear at the centre of an English novel and, significantly, one of the first anti-heroes – a brief, shabby, confused life and a violent, accidental death, a man robbed of his birthright but unable to name the thief.

If it suited employers to hire hands only rather than eyes and minds as well, then clearly education could be a threat to them – for it might develop the eyes to see and the minds to understand what struck Stephen Blackpool as an incomprehensible muddle. The employers and their representatives realised that. A magistrate noted in 1807: 'It is doubtless desirable that the poor should be instructed in *reading*, if it were only for the best of purposes – that they may read the Scriptures. As to *writing* and *arithmetic*, it may be apprehended that such a circle of knowledge would produce in them a disrelish for the laborious occupations of life.'

It was attitudes like this that made reformers determined to equip the hands – the Wombles required by the bosses – with eyes and minds. The campaign for mass education succeeded in bringing schooling to everyone by the end of the nineteenth century. This was a tremendous advance, but it failed to bring real insight and understanding along with it. Part of the reason why can be glimpsed in Richard Altick's *The English Common Reader: a Social History of The Mass Reading Public, 1800–1900*. Looking back from 1957 on the growth of literacy, he concludes:

> The long hours and the monotony of work in factory and shop, the dismal surroundings in which people were condemned to spend such leisure as they had, the regimentation of industrial society with its consequent crushing of individuality, made it imperative that the English millions should have some way of escape and

relaxation, some new and plentiful means of engaging their minds and imaginations. Books and periodicals were the obvious answer.

If we pull one word out of that liberal piety, it all falls down. 'Imperative.' Why imperative? Imperative for whom? . . . Precisely! Altick goes on:

> Though in the first half of the century there was deep (and not wholly idle) apprehension that making the 'lower ranks' of society literate would breed all sorts of disorder and debauchery, in the long run the proliferation of reading matter proved to have been the oil that was needed to quiet the troubled waters . . . The comparative tranquility of Victorian society after the mid-century was due in no small part to the growth of the popular press.

One of the editors of that popular press, James Payn of *Chambers Journal*, put this argument in a nutshell in the 1860s: 'Books are the blessed chloroform of the mind.' Educate the hand's mind if that's what he wants, but let's make sure that mind stays asleep.

With the growth of mass literacy came the growth of mass pulp to absorb and deflect that literacy. The Religious Tract Society claimed that it set up the *Boys' Own Paper* in 1879 'to illustrate by practical example the noblest type of manhood and truest Christian devotion.' It was soon selling a quarter of a million copies a week. *Tit-Bits* and the *Daily Mail* followed; heavily supported by advertisers, they were both selling over half a million copies per issue by the end of the century. What Orwell later called the dictatorship of the chocolate manufacturers had arrived.

By that time also sections of the working class had won the right to vote and so the survival of the system became dependent on their support. It therefore became essential to train workers to accept the values of that system and all it stands for. Education became not liberation but drilling in servility, as two of the most acute late Victorian authors pointed out. In his novel *The Way of All Flesh*, Samuel Butler observes gloomily of one of his characters that 'by far the greater part . . . of his education had been an attempt, not so much to keep him in blinkers as to gouge his eyes out altogether.' In Oscar Wilde's play *The Importance of Being Earnest*, Lady Bracknell remarks: 'Fortunately in England, at any rate, education produces no effect whatsoever. If it did, it would prove a serious danger to the upper classes, and probably lead to acts of violence in Grosvenor Square.' Readers may remember that in 1968 there were signs that education in England *was* beginning to produce an effect and there were indeed acts of violence in Grosvenor Square. Since then it's noticeable that the upper classes have decided that lots of shiny new universities are certainly not a help in solving the problems of British capitalism, though it's a solution that a lot of their hopes were pinned on in the early sixties.

What Dickens, then, had sensed through the figure of Stephen Blackpool was the way that capitalism didn't need people, it only needed hands. People are awkward. In large numbers they tend to form mobs and make policemen work overtime. But hands are harmless. They have no voices and if properly trained can make a lot of money for the man who hires them. Stephen Blackpool embodies a whole analysis of nineteenth century capitalist society, of the way that society rose on sweated manual labour and how it thought of its basis as 'the hands'.

In the twentieth century the process of automation has replaced many of the hands. The focus of exploitation has shifted but exploitation itself remains, and so too do the partial human beings to service and staff it. Capitalist society now tries to preserve itself with a precariously interlocking and frantically stimulated system of greeds and so it encourages people to think of themselves primarily as consumers living in a consumer society.

Consumers. It's worth thinking about the term because it's what we're asked to call ourselves. No longer just hands but instead a sort of huge corporate mouth into which pours a spectacular stream of glossy crap. We're invited to join a Consumers' Association. There have been Ministers for Consumer Affairs. 'But what about the consumer?', demands the trendy BBC interviewer of some harassed trade unionist who's gone on strike and interrupted the flow of glossy crap.

It's imperative – imperative for them – that we should think of ourselves simply as consumers. If you think of yourself simply as a consumer, simply as a mouth, in that one-dimensional way, then of course you oppose strikes. Strikes interrupt the flow of consumer goods. Strikes are bad for consumers. Strikes should be outlawed. But if you think of yourself as more than a consumer, if you think of yourself in multi-dimensional terms – as a worker, a father, a mother, a human being and so on – then you might identify with that harassed glossy crap-packer on the box, you might see his problems as your problems too. You might support his strike.

Hands in the nineteenth century, consumers in the twentieth. What will we be next? Knees? Left armpits? Nostrils? Who knows? Nobody yet, though there's probably an adman somewhere with a shrewd idea. It's clear that the system doesn't like the full you but is happy to use and plug away at any temporarily profitable part. The full you could be a complex nuisance but the partial you is pretty easy to handle. Dickens suggests as much in a scene in Chapter 11 of *Hard Times*. Stephen Blackpool the power-loom weaver meets Mr Bounderby, his boss:

> 'Now, you know,' said Mr Bounderby, taking some sherry, 'we have never had any difficulty with you, and you have never been one of the unreasonable ones. You don't expect to be set up in a coach and six, and to be fed on turtle soup and venison, with a gold spoon, as a good many of 'em do!' Mr Bounderby always represented this to be the sole, immediate, and direct object of any Hand who was not entirely satisfied; 'and therefore I know already that you have not come here to make a complaint. Now, you know, I am certain of that, beforehand.'
>
> 'No, sir, sure I ha' not coom for nowt o' th' kind.'

Mr Bounderby seemed agreeably surprised, notwithstanding his previous strong conviction. 'Very well,' he returned. 'You're a steady Hand, and I was not mistaken.'

And so Stephen, isolated and bewildered, not a full human being but just a steady hand, wanders off and drops down a hole. Isolated, bewildered hands often did. Isolated bewildered consumers often will. But what happens when the Wombles come back out of their holes and stop living off scraps of rubbish? If they could see themselves as full human beings they might want the whole bloody Common.

9. WILLIAM SHAKESPEARE AND MORE ORIGINAL SIN

If you read one of Shakespeare's tragedies at school the odds are you were asked to spend a lot of time in class talking about what they call the hero's tragic flaw – that fault in his character which brings about his downfall. The immaturity of Romeo, the procrastination of Hamlet, the jealousy of Othello, the ambition of Macbeth – these are the weaknesses, so the story goes, which in the end draw these people to their deaths. Interpretation of this kind is very common. There are two other things that need saying about it: it's extremely reactionary and it has nothing to do with Shakespeare. How has this irrelevant notion taken root and why is it clamped on most people's minds as soon as they pick up Shakespeare's work?

The idea of the tragic flaw has obvious religious appeal. A socialist poet once pointed out:

> Religion never has you faltering
> In the belief that you not they need altering.

In other words when the religious mind is confronted with a mess – especially the kind of mess we find at the end of Shakespearean tragedy with the stage covered with dead bodies – its natural reaction is not to look for structural causes but rather to beat its breast and cry: 'Let us root out the evil in our own hearts!' In literary terms this means blaming the mess at the end of Shakespearean tragedy not on some sort of clash between the hero and his world but rather on the evil in the hero's heart, his tragic flaw. Thus the notion of tragic flaw becomes a kind of literary equivalent of our old favourite, original sin.

Once you can get readers and audiences to behave like apprentice Grand Inquisitors sniffing round for a scent of the hero's sin, lists of those sins are fairly easy to make. The literary critic Wilson Knight, for example, assures us that the something rotten in the state of Denmark is Hamlet himself. Schoolchildren all over the world have therefore been solemnly informed that Hamlet's tragic flaw is indecision. The Ghost tells him to kill his stepfather but he can't bring himself to act. Murdering when ordered to do so by an authoritative father figure is, it would appear, a quality we would like to see developed in all our young men, so Hamlet stands as a sort of glum moral warning about what happens when this quality is found wanting.

Critics make the same sort of maniacal nonsense of most of the rest of the tragedies. Othello's tragic flaw? Jealousy, says F.R.Leavis. Macbeth's? That's an easy one: ambition, says A.C.Bradley. Antony's? Sexual passion, says Derek Traversi. And so on.

To turn from this to the Marxist approach. What the Marxist tries to do is avoid lumbering the work with dogmatic categories like tragic flaw. Instead he attempts to make sense of it with analysis that is in the first place sociological. By this I mean that he tries to understand the work not in the light of someone's bright – or highly slanted – idea but by placing the work in that actual society where it belongs and where it developed. He tries to see the work not through lenses designed by Bradley or Leavis but in the context of the moment when it first appeared.

Okay, that's the theory, but what does it mean in practice? It means that in order to grasp what's going on in a particular work we must first try to understand the particular situation in which the work was written. It's convenient for educational institutions to split reality up into separate departments - English; Politics; Geography; Engineering;

Basket Weaving and so on – but the world doesn't exist in convenient boxes. To understand any one object – like, for example a play by Shakespeare – we have to try and break these boxes down and see how the particular object relates to and grows out of its whole world.

About Shakespeare's world we need to say three things, however briefly. First, he lived in an age of sharp transition when feudalism was finally falling apart – the Rising of the Northern Earls in 1569 when Shakespeare was 5 is normally described by historians as feudalism's last bid for power – and in an age when the pre-conditions for capitalist society were being laid. Secondly, out of the decay of feudalism and the possibilities that opened up, there was an explosive growth of confidence in human abilities and in the capacities of the human mind that expressed itself in literature as the Elizabethan Renaissance. That literature is full of delight in men and women, in their qualities and liberated individualities. Hamlet's famous lines 'What a piece of work is a man! How noble in reason! how infinite in faculties! in form and moving, how express and admirable! in action, how like an angel! in apprehension, how like a god! the beauty of the world! the paragon of animals!' could not have been imagined by the medieval mind, obsessed as it was by a sense of man's fallen nature. Shakespeare's three dozen plays with their armies of rich characters are together an impressive celebration of human potential freed, or apparently beginning to be freed, by the struggles of sixteenth and seventeeth century history.

Thirdly, the theatre Shakespeare wrote for was a new, capitalist theatre. In other words it worked by charging people for admission and making a profit. Capitalism at first means an immense expansion of the possible. Before the 1570s dramatic performances were infrequent, usually put on for a small elite in one of the great houses. The dramatist was dependent for his livelihood on pleasing aristocratic patrons – which often meant producing what Orwell calls 'revolting flatteries'. With the building of commercial theatres a dozen or so years before Shakespeare started his career, plays could now be aimed at a much wider public – at the penny-a-timers in the pit as well as at the seated gentry. This meant new prospects, much wider horizons, and was another liberating force.

What does all this mean for Shakespeare's tragedies? First, it means massive, highly individualised characters, the first of their kind in literature. Into these characters Shakespeare projects contemporary dreams of total self-realisation. His characters exploit the possibilities that the newly glimpsed freedoms seem to offer. But tragedy in Shakespeare springs again and again from the clash between men and women awakened, men and women battling to fulfil themselves, and Shakespeare's sense, shaped by his times, of the very tiny room for genuine self-realisation that the world actually offers. Again and again Shakespearean tragedy agonises over this contradiction: the fragile beauty of Romeo and Juliet smothered by the feudal vendettas of Verona; the limitless mind of Hamlet clogged in the rotten state of Denmark; the noble Othello wrecked in a racist society, Antony and Cleopatra in a militarist one.[1]

Tragedy in Shakespeare therefore springs not from the hero's flaw or sin but from his dislocation, his attempt to live in ways that his society suggests but does not yet accept. So, for example, Macbeth and his wife are desperate to climb a rung higher on the social ladder, a desire which capitalist society has since come to insist on as the motor of all human progress. But they do not live in a socially mobile world; theirs is a feudal one where you are born into a certain station and stay there. Out of that contradiction grows their tragedy.

Or take Romeo and Juliet. They want to choose their own marriage partners. This is now recognised as a basic human right. But they live in a society which doesn't recognise that right and which gives Juliet's father the right to dump her in the lap of the highest bidder. Again, out of that dislocation comes the tragedy. It's a sense of dislocation that was a common experience for Shakespeare and his contemporaries, living as they did with the muddle of feudalism gone senile and capitalism only half born. 'If wee present a mingle-mangle,' wrote John Lyly in a much quoted passage, 'our fault is to be excused, because the whole worlde is become an Hodge-podge.'

The point I'm trying to make will I think be clearer if we play a game. Imagine you're writing a tragic drama about the life and death of Christ, based on the Bible story. Forget all the religious nonsense: you're going to take him as the usual tragic hero, the impressive character who gets destroyed at the end.

What's going to be the tragic flaw in your hero? It'd be easy to make a list. You could make him a naive idealist, like Romeo, unable to come to terms with the real world. Or you could suggest that he's indecisive, like Hamlet, dithering about in the Garden of Gethsemane and missing the chance to save himself. Then again you could say he's ambitious, like Macbeth, with grandiose schemes for saving the world. Or, like Othello, he's liable to violent outbursts of passion as when he takes a whip to the buyers and sellers in the Temple.

A play written and understood in these terms would have at least two results. First, the real crooks get off scot free. Christ gets nailed up because of his own weaknesses, not because of Judas, the Pharisees and the Roman authorities. Second, the story is castrated. If you see someone being crucified and conclude that it's his own fault then you can shrug your shoulders, say sorry and get on with the gardening. But if, on the other hand, someone basically decent is getting nailed up then the effect on you, the beholder, is disturbing. If decent people are getting nailed up then clearly it's not the best of all possible worlds you live in. 'If it can happen to *him* then who's safe? Maybe things need changing. . . .'

What's important to learn from this game is that, once you accept the terms of a given question, you are trapped into giving certain answers. Only by challenging the question can you break out of the blinkers it carries with it. Buy the notion of tragic flaw and you see the plays in a distorted but convincing way. Hamlet dies because he procrastinates, you say, forgetting the real villains, the murderous Claudius, the spying Polonius, the corrupt state of Denmark. Othello dies because he's jealous, you add, ignoring the plots of Iago, the prejudice of Brabantio, the racism of Venice.

It's a crucial stage in education when you stop answering the questions your teachers set and start asking your own. If you accept their questions – for example, how are we going to save British capitalism? – you're half way to accepting their answers – wage restraint and unemployment. Only by rejecting their question which reflects their priorities and substituting your own can you start getting at the truth.

To conclude: tragedy is subversive. It undermines our sense of living in the best of all possible worlds by showing us good people getting screwed. Schools aren't in business to teach subversive literature so they stand Shakespeare on his head. You can begin by putting him the right way up.

---

[1] This paragraph derives in part from Chapter IV of Christopher Caudwell's *Illusion and Reality*.

10. CAPITALISM, COMPETITION AND KING LEAR

Competition, they tell us, makes the world go round. It's the reason for the appearance of most things from better mousetraps to longer long jumpers. Its presence is the basis of a free society, its absence is why the National Coal Board makes a loss. As long as we each spend our time trying to knock lumps off one another then, apparently, a great civilisation is assured. So beaver about looking after yourself, tread on anyone who gets in the way and we'll soon put the Great back into Britain. The need for greater efficiency and higher profitability means that those who compete well must be rewarded and those who fail can go and hang themselves. In 1967 Reginald Maudling, the Tory politician who later was to become a world famous failure himself, put this whole argument in terms that may be taken as typical:

> We must constantly encourage competition not simply because it is the best safeguard for the consumer but because if competition dies away so the spirit of pride and endeavour will die with it. Then we must change the tax system which at present bears so heavily upon success, particularly individual success. . . .
>
> Finally, there must be penalties too, because the spirit we require to see will not be fully forthcoming unless we ally a proper regard for success with a proper acceptance of the consequences of failure.
>
> *The Times*, October 7, 1967.

Competition, in short, means rewards for the rich, penalties for the rest and a better tomorrow for all.

Reginald Maudling, of course, is a fool whereas William Shakespeare was not, so that when Shakespeare came to write a play about a competitive society he saw such a society as tragic. The play's called *King Lear*, and since cant about competition shows little sign of withering away it's a play that's well worth a look.

Lear's story was several hundred years old by the time Shakespeare took it up – a simple, well-known folk tale. In its earliest versions it told of a king who asks his three daughters how much they love him. The two older girls flatter him with flowery declarations, the youngest says simply that she loves him as meat loves salt. Furious, the king drives her away but later comes to learn the value of salt and is reconciled to her.

Shakespeare takes hold of this thin material, and alters and expands it to make it convey his ideas fully. First he joins it with a story of a struggle between the Duke of Gloucester and his two sons, Edmund and Edgar. Hence the battles in the Lear family become not eccentric, the result of one old man's whim, but rather one more sign of widespread social tension. Second and above all he changes the end of the story to make it tragic. Goneril, the oldest sister, stabs herself after poisoning her sister Regan. Cordelia, the youngest of the three girls, is hanged and Lear dies in despair. The reasons for these radical changes will emerge if we look at the play in a bit of detail.

Lear's Britain as presented at the start of the play is a feudal society with a rigid hierarchy dominated by two old families, King Lear's and the Duke of Gloucester's. Lear decides to dismantle that society and set up a competitive one in its place. He decides that his successor will not be his firstborn, as feudal custom would demand. Instead he sets up a competition between his three daughters. 'Which of you shall we say doth love us most?', he asks them, intending to reward the one who answers best and impose what Reginald Maudling calls 'the consequences of failure' on the rest. Goneril and Regan compete effectively and get half the kingdom each; Cordelia refuses to play silly games and is thrown out.

After giving away his kingdom, Lear hopes to retain nominal power based on the traditional duties owed to him by his two ruling daughters. However, as his court jester the Fool points out, by getting rid of his property he has lost all claim to proper regard in the new society that's coming into being. This is a society that respects those who accumulate with competitive ferocity and one which, ironically, Lear himself had helped to create with his love competition in the opening scene. In such a society, Cordelia's love expressed in formal, feudal terms ('I love your Majesty/According to my bond') counts for nothing, and characters who continue to act out of the old loyalties are forced into hiding and disguise. Lear is treated with increasing contempt as a boring irrelevance by Goneril and Regan. This contempt, by the middle of the play, drives him mad.

The crudest representative of the new order is Edmund, Gloucester's 'illegitimate' son in the terms of the old society and now in the new society quite ready to sell out his father in order to get his hands on 'that which my father loses'. He chases after power in the form of property with a ruthlessness that cuts right through family ties. Thus he first slanders and so secures the disinheritance of his brother Edgar. Then he betrays the efforts of his father Gloucester to comfort the rejected Lear, a betrayal which leads Regan first to tear out Gloucester's eyes in punishment and then to hand over his estates to Edmund. Thus Gloucester begins to see the cruelty of the new order as it blinds him just as Lear had begun to understand its insanity as it drove him mad. A world that you must be mad to understand and blind to see: it's through these bitter paradoxes that Shakespeare expressed what he sensed would be the development of the post-feudal, competitive society that was erupting around him.

I hesitate to say that Shakespeare shows the new society eventually perishing in its own contradictions because that sounds a bit glib, yet in fact that's more or less what happens. On a simple level, anyone who has played the game 'Monopoly' knows that at first the competitive element benefits most of the players but soon they're trying to bankrupt each other in order to survive. Similarly, Lear sets up a competitive society in the first scene and those who, like Regan, have no scruples about stamping on people's eyeballs, prosper hugely for a while. But soon the competition to continue has to feed on itself. Before the play's half over we hear of 'likely wars' between the husbands of Goneril and Regan. By the last scene Edmund, himself wounded and dying after a fight with his brother, is left to note how Goneril and Regan wiped each other out in the struggle for his affections: The one the other poisoned for my sake/And after slew herself.' As the competitive society collapses in on itself it orders, as a last obscene gesture, the hanging of the innocent Cordelia, an action that causes Lear to die of a broken heart.

What we get, in short, in the second half of the play is a grotesque vision of the future of capitalist society in which, in the words of Goneril's husband Albany, 'Humanity must perforce prey on itself, /Like monsters of the deep.' Kenneth Muir's edition of the play comments on these words: 'There are many parallels in contemporary and preceding literature', and goes on to refer to half a dozen sixteenth and seventeenth century examples. Clearly when Shakespeare through Albany describes Lear's society in these cannibal terms he's expressing a view which many echoed and which therefore points beyond the limits of the play itself to Shakespeare's own radically disturbed world.

Most teachers of English would not accept this account of *King Lear*. The consensus is that Art deals with Eternal Verities (here all genuflect), with Abiding Truths about Man and Nature. It has little to do with fiddling things like politics or the rise of capitalism or the ownership of theatres or whatever it is that Marxists try and read into it. On the contrary, it captures an Unchanging Human Essence. That is why it appeals to all men in all ages – why, indeed, audiences in the age of astronauts and H-bombs still go to see a play like *Lear* written in an age of maypoles and muskets.

This argument, or more sophisticated versions of it, can fairly be described as the ideological core of most of the teaching of literature. It's also the point where the Marxist approach meets strongest resistance – resistance because the Marxist insists on seeing men and women as constantly involved in a process of change, changing their societies and their environment and, through that, changing themselves, their nature and eventually their art too. If you see human history this way it doesn't leave much room for eternal verities and genuflection.

The proof of the pudding is in the eating. The only way we can decide between these two approaches is not through sterile debate but rather by looking at what actually happens in the real world. That means, in the present case, looking at what has happened to *King Lear*.

The play has had an odd history. Shakespeare wrote it about 370 years ago, around 1605. In 1681 a hack called Nahum Tate took hold of it and radically rewrote it. Crucially, he gave it what he called 'Regularity and Probability' by supplying a happy ending in which Lear is put back on the throne and Cordelia gets married. Tate's version became popular and Shakespeare's play disappeared from the stage for 160 years and didn't return till 1838. A curious thing for a work to do if, as it's claimed, it appeals to all men in all ages. Why did this happen?

I argued in the first half of this chapter that in *King Lear* Shakespeare sees feudalism dying and watches capitalism's bloody birth. He sees the new forces of capitalism and especially its competitive basis as in the end monstrous and tragic. But 1681, when Tate's *Lear* succeeds Shakespeare's, marks the start of a violent decade in which capitalism takes important steps to establish itself. The crushing of Monmouth's rebellion in 1685, the so-called Glorious Revolution and the dethroning of King James II in 1688, and William's victory over James at the Battle of the Boyne in 1690 are some of those steps. The Glorious Revolution changed English society. It made the crown a clearly circumscribed, bourgeois monarchy, deprived of control over the army and the judges. It set up the Bank of England and instituted the National Debt, thus laying the basis for the development of full-scale capitalism. A society moving rapidly in a direction Shakespeare defined as blind and mad would find his play bewildering and remote. It preferred the 'Regularity and Probability' of Tate's happy version.

Tate's play held the stage throughout the eighteenth century. Dr. Johnson, the most perceptive of eighteenth century critics, remarked in 1765 that 'in the present case the public has decided. Cordelia, from the time of Tate, has always retired with victory and felicity.' He adds that his own judgment falls in with 'the general suffrage.'

Early nineteenth century critics, though responding like Dr Johnson to bits and pieces of Shakespeare's play, generally agreed with Dr. Johnson's verdict. Charles Lamb, for example, noted in 1811 that 'the Lear of Shakespeare cannot be acted.'

But in the eighteen thirties things began to change profoundly and with those changes Shakespeare's *Lear* began to be seen differently. In 1834, less than ten years after the legalisation of trade unions, the Grand National Consolidated Trades Union was formed and announced 'a different order of things' as one of its main aims. In 1837 the Chartists, described by A. L. Morton as 'the first independent political party of the working class', were launched. In 1839 there's the first recorded use of the word 'socialism' in the English language.

The eighteen thirties then is clearly that decade in English history when at theoretical, organisational and even linguistic levels capitalist society is first radically called into question. For the first time many men and women saw capitalism not as some inevitable, natural order but as something that human beings had imposed and that human beings at last really stood a good chance of changing. And so for the first time they began to organise to bring about that change. Capitalism in the eighteen thirties was no longer just permanently there, like the weather. It suddenly became problematic and replaceable.

At such a moment Shakespeare's *Lear*, which intuitively senses and acts out the tragedy and absurdity of capitalist principles, would speak to people, however subconsciously, in ways that it hadn't for generations. So in 1838 William Macready produced it on the London stage and it's remained there, on and off, ever since.

11. COPPERS' TRUNCHEONS AND HAPPY ENDINGS

A few years ago my kids brought a couple of books home from the library and I settled down to read to them. The first one was about a sad donkey – sad because he had long funny ears. They kept catching on barbed wire, tripping him up, getting in his breakfast and generally making the rest of the donkeys bray with laughter. The donkey tried everything: tying them in a knot, turning them inside out, visiting a quack vet, but it was no use. Tears rolled down his face. Then one day along came a lady donkey who just adored long ears. She fell in love with the sad donkey, cheered him up, and soon they were married and lived happily ever after.

The second story was about a goldfish. He was browned off too – bored out of his mind in a garden pond swimming round the same cement gnome every day. So one night he popped into the overflow pipe, down the drain and out to sea in search of adventure. His mum and dad were against it and preferred to stay at home watching *Coronation St*. The sea turned out a disaster: cold, dark salty and full of miserable crabs. Tears rolled down the goldfish's face. Then one day he found himself swimming past the end of a familiar drain. Up he went, along the overflow pipe and pop! back into the old familiar little pond. Mum and Dad were overjoyed, the goldfish never grumbled about boredom again and lived happily ever after.

Two different stories and harmless slabs of plastic in themselves, but it's amazing when you stop and listen how often the same pattern and the same message get repeated. Your world and your position in it might seem dismal but they're as good as you'll get so there's no point in doing anything about it. If you do try and improve it then either, like the donkey, you're wasting your time or, like the goldfish, you'll only make matters worse. So leave things as they are, be grateful for what you've got, do as you're told, and in the end you'll learn to love it all. P.S. Support your local moderate candidates.

Bosses' propaganda comes in all shapes and sizes. You don't have to have property developers as heroes and anarcho-syndicalist shop stewards with strong Trotskyite tendencies as villains to get your point across. Often what's crucial is not who the characters are – who is hero and who is villain, though this may be relevant. More important are the values that the novel or film or TV show acts out or condemns, and how those values relate to our society and the various sections and classes within it.

In short, as Orwell once pointed out, all art is propaganda. He later expanded the remark a bit: 'Every artist is a propagandist in the sense that he is trying, directly or indirectly, to impose a vision of life that seems to him desirable.'[1] It's impossible to disagree with this. You can't string two phrases together without your values beginning to come into play. The fact that I'm writing these particular words and not other ones is the result of all sorts of value judgments going on in the back of my head, selecting, rejecting, ordering, shaping. And this remains true whether you're writing a poem about Spring or a pamphlet about workers' control.

If values penetrate what we read and see in this way, then it's worth stopping to think for a minute about some of the forms those values take. Once you can recognise them, half the battle is won, because you've got your own built-in crap detector, able to spot and filter out some of the traditional devices of social control. Here, let's take just two

81

of the most widespread forms: propaganda directed at children and the propaganda value of happy endings.

Propaganda for children is usually pretty crude. If you've forgotten how crude, spend five minutes listening to the mind-smashing, down-on-your-knees religious drivel that gets talked at the average school assembly and you'll soon remember. Even the games children play are often sabotaged by the prejudices of their elders. So, for example, a well researched television play a couple of years ago called *The Death of Adolf Hitler* featured Dr Goebbels's children playing a 'Snakes and Ladders' type of game called 'Get the Jews'. The seven year old winner 'got' 45,000, to Eva Braun's applause. Trust the Nazis to poison even the kids' minds. And yet most of us were brought up on Cowboys and Indians. There's no getting round the fact that the game re-enacts and celebrates the genocide that was the basis of the American empire. Of course it's a fantastic game for children in terms of its *form*: it's exciting, it's full of movement, it lets them in imagination remake themselves and their world and so on. But the problem is the *content* of the game. It's possible to have others with these same qualities, but the one capitalism overwhelmingly offers and reinforces with comics and films is reducing lots of brown people to pulp or herding them in concentration camps called reservations.

When Walt Disney Inc is not busy making money in this way out of the roots of American imperialism it's busy cultivating its branches. *Disney Landia*, a comic published in Chile seven months after the Fascist coup of September 1973, pictures helpless kittens attacked by two vultures called Hegel and Marx. As a farmer drives them off with a shotgun, Jiminy Cricket comments with delight: 'Ha! Fire-arms are the only things these bloody birds are afraid of.'[2] You're liable to be sent to prison if you show children pictures of people making love. Show them pictures of people making mincemeat of Commies and Redskins and you're liable to make a lot of money.

What about happy endings? It was argued earlier that the effect of tragedy is subversive in so far as it presents to us characters we learn to admire and then shows them being nailed up, something that would not happen if their society were just. The device of the happy ending reverses this pattern. We are shown characters with all sorts of problems, but in the end, like the donkey we started with, they manage to find a way around them and live happily ever after. If all problems are surmountable with a bit of luck and effort then clearly no radical changes are necessary.

This sort of structure is very common in the Victorian novel. For example Dickens in *Hard Times* is very perceptive about some of the human mutilations that nineteenth century capitalism was responsible for. But in the end Dickens, like all good liberals, backs away from the full implications of his own criticisms. Hence organisations like trade unions that try to defend people from those mutilations are presented as the worthless tools of an outside agitator called Slackbridge. A bit of crude juggling and Dickens conjures up a last page soggy not just with pie in the sky but rather with soggy pie for all, right here and now:

> But, happy Sissy's happy children loving her; all children loving her; she, grown learned in childish lore; thinking no innocent and pretty fancy ever to be despised; trying hard to know her humbler fellow-creatures, and to beautify their lives of machinery and reality with those imaginative graces and delights, without which the heart of infancy will wither up, the sturdiest physical manhood will be morally stark death, and the plainest national prosperity figures can show, will be the Writing on the Wall, – she holding this as part of no fantastic vow, or bond, or brotherhood, or sisterhood, or pledge, or covenant, or fancy dress, or fancy fair; but simply as a duty to be done, – did Louisa see these things of herself? These things were to be.

There's an obvious connection in these two curious sentences between the sheer dishonesty – part wishful thinking, part misrepresentation – of what's being said and the fantastically crabbed, convoluted, lopsided, twisting and roundabout way it's being said.

George Bernard Shaw may often have been a fool in his old age but this shouldn't be allowed to detract from the sharpness of his early plays. In his very first, *Widowers' Houses*, written in 1892, he takes a hatchet to the rotten device of the happy ending. Dr Trench the hero wants to marry Sartorius's daughter Blanche but is horrified to find that the family's money comes from the extortionate rents of slum tenants. However it's soon revealed that his own handsome private income comes in fact from interest on a mortgage he holds on some of Sartorius's slum properties. Sartorius milks his tenants in order to keep up with the monthly payments due to Dr Trench. Collapse of Trench's stout liberal scruples, which by the end have declined to a few cynical observations as he exits to marriage and happiness ever after with Blanche.

In Victorian novel after Victorian novel – and indeed later in Hollywood film after Hollywood film – the heroine is swept off by the hero in the closing moments to what Orwell once called 'a sort of radiant idleness' – independent means, roses round the cottage door and on the children's cheeks, and a loyal working-class lunatic in the background to cook the meals, wash the floors and provide comic relief when she drops her aitches or the spoons. Shaw is one of the first to ask rude questions about the economic basis of this fairy tale and to point out that it doesn't happen in a social vacuum. If some people in the end are able to put their feet up for the rest of their lives it's because some people elsewhere are being screwed to generate the cash.

It's necessary to be careful at this point or else you can end up arguing that for art to be progressive it has to be bloody miserable, and that anything that gives us half a smile is part of a ruling class plot to convince us that we live in the best of all possible worlds. But it certainly *is* true that when serious artists have tried to describe a state of genuine happiness .- genuine happiness as opposed to limp little bourgeois dreams of sitting about twiddling your thumbs and watching the roses and the savings account grow – they have been forced to present that happiness existing in spite of or outside their particular world.

Shakespeare, for example, knew that in his world, as in *King Lear*, people tended to get their eyeballs trodden on, so that when he wants his characters to enjoy themselves, to stretch their minds and their emotions and their potentials to the limits, he shifts them into a deliberately unreal place – an enchanted wood in *Midsummer Night's Dream*, a Bohemian harvest festival in *The Winter's Tale*, a magic island in *The Tempest*. In this last play the hero Prospero literally waves a magic wand and freezes for the moment all the life-denying forces in violently emerging capitalist society. So it is that his daughter Miranda is able to gaze around in wonder and exclaim:

> How many goodly creatures are there here!
> How beauteous mankind is! O brave new world,
> That has such people in it!

In the twentieth century, after another four hundred years of human, social and technical development, it's central to the socialist case that you don't need a magic wand any more to catch a glimpse of a brave new world. For the first time it's something that we really can make together. So we need to see clearly that novels and films that nihilistically deny that possibility or that suggest that life's better under the Conservatives and so doesn't need tinkering with are the soft ideological equivalent of the policeman's truncheon – weapons for keeping people in their places and preserving things as they are.

---

[1] *Collected Essays, Journalism and Letters*, Vol.ii, p.41.

[2] Reprinted in *Chile Fights*, London June–July 1974.

12. SUPERMAN, THE SEVEN GATES OF THEBES, AND YOU

What everyone in this country is agreed on is our need for firm and decisive leadership at the top, the *Daily Mail* said recently. (The *Daily Mail* uses the word 'everyone' a lot, but in its own distinct way. Roughly translated into English it seems to mean 'the *Daily Mail*'.) We used to have such leadership and then the country did alright. Now we don't have any and the place is in a mess. We last had firm and decisive leadership during the Second World War. Its name was Winston Churchill and it worked wonders. Here is a typical recent assessment of it, in the Preface to Patrick Cosgrave's *Churchill at War*: 'The book is, in the author's view, the story of how Churchill had defeated Germany by the end of 1940.'

Defeating the Nazis singlehanded inside a year with no apparent help from all you idle mob out there is, you will agree, something of a feat, and not something any of our present lot of politicians could be trusted to repeat. Everyone (i.e. the *Daily Mail*) used to think Enoch might be the man. But then he suggested voting Labour so everyone (i.e. ditto) went off him a bit and we're back at square one, looking for a leader to put the country back on its feet and the workers back on their knees. Without one we're sunk.

The middle classes and their spokesmen do tend to go on a bit about the sanctity and supremacy of the individual but when it comes to the crunch they appear to regard the individual and indeed the whole mass of individuals as irrelevant. All you really need is one Great Man. In fact all history, I once heard a university lecturer insist, is the history of Great Men. Hence the present spate of calls for a leader, a Great Man, to take up the reins of history and get Britain moving again.

Meanwhile the job of all of the rest of us is to be silent spectators, waiting for a Great Man to come along and tell us to jump to it. The novelist William Golding put it this way:

> New ages, new schools, new floods of literature do not emerge by a process of gradualism from what went before. Nor are major changes in awareness merely the work of economics or even the accumulation of knowledge. They have always come in the first place through the medium of one man.
>
> *Times Literary Supplement*, June 17, 1960.

In a sense this is slightly consoling for us men, because it does suggest that once an epoch at least one of us makes a decent contribution. But it seems from this that you ladies have contributed bugger all since history began. Useless lot of parasites. Never mind, keep ironing the shirts and you'll get your reward in the next world.

A generation ago the German writer Bertolt Brecht answered all the above rubbish in a poem called 'A Worker Reads History'. This is it.

> Who built the seven gates of Thebes?
> The books are filled with the names of Kings.
> Was it Kings who hauled the craggy blocks of stone?
> And Babylon, so many times destroyed,
> Who built the city up each time? In which of Lima's houses
> That city glittering with gold, lived those who built it?
> In the evening when the Chinese wall was finished
> Where did the masons go? Imperial Rome
> Is full of arcs of triumph. Who reared them up? Over whom
> Did the Caesars triumph? Byzantium lives in song,
> Were all her dwellings palaces? And even in Atlantis of the legend
> The night the sea rushed in,
> The drowning men still bellowed for their slaves.

Young Alexander conquered India
He alone?
Caesar beat the Gauls
Was there not even a cook in his army?
Philip of Spain wept as his fleet
Was sunk and destroyed. Were there no other tears?
Frederick the Great triumphed in the Seven Years' War. Who
Triumphed with him?

Each page a victory,
At whose expense the victory ball?
Every ten years a great man,
Who paid the piper?

So many particulars
So many questions.

Quoted in
Ken Coates and Richard Silburn
Poverty: The Forgotten Englishmen
Penguin 1970, p.23.

Enough said. Even at the lowest level, a poem like this can give you a good laugh the next time a TV quizmaster assures you that, say, Edward the Confessor built Westminster Abbey or Nelson won the Battle of Trafalgar or Stephenson made the first locomotive.

The poem also raises questions about how history is made and who makes it. A way of answering those questions is to look at another example. Everyone knows, as the *Daily Mail* might say, that Sir Humphry Davy invented the miners' safety lamp, thus singlehandedly saving thousands of lives and earning the miners' eternal gratitude (in so far as miners, a graceless lot, are capable of gratitude.) Yet push past this myth and you find Dave Douglass in *Pit Life in County Durham* describing the miners' 'stubborn refusal to adopt the Davy lamp which continued until late in the nineteenth century.' You find that miners disliked the Davy lamp for two good reasons. First, its light was in the early years much poorer than the traditional candles. So it cut heavily into the miners' earnings because in the gloom they loaded more stone in with the coal and hence had more confiscated from their wages by the mine owners. Secondly, the new lamp meant, so the owners insisted, that places previously too dangerous to work by the light of naked flames could now be tackled and were to be tackled. At once, deaths by suffocation and gassing began to rise, so that far from saving miners' lives there were in fact *more* deaths in the coalfields in the years immediately after the introduction of the Davy lamp than in the years before.

Thinking about the story of the Davy lamp you begin to get a glimpse of how history really works. Out goes the toiling, lonely genius making a brilliant discovery and changing the lives of a thick and sleepy people. Instead you see peoples' lives and work uncovering problems, solutions tried, tested by mass experience, found wanting, resisted, adapted, tried again, changed again, fought against, modified, fought for and finally accepted. The men digging underground today live marginally safer lives not because of a Great Man but because behind them lie the experience, the skills and the militancy of millions of miners and their organisations over generations. It's these things which have shaped the miners' history and the conditions under which they work. What's true for the miners is true for the rest of us too.

What's true for the rest of us is not true of the comics we were offered as kids. Our role in the Superman sort of comic is that of innocent bystander, helpless and panic stricken, incapable of doing anything against Mandrill or the Thing from Planet X or whatever. We're only saved when Superman strips down to his Y-fronts and gets to work. Superman hits all problems on the jaw and they go away, so happily we can carry on living exactly the same sort of lives as before without the need for any radical, disturbing changes.

Turn to cowboy films and the pattern is the same.

Gary Cooper, John Wayne and Henry Fonda are three of the best known cowboy actors, and three of their most famous films were, respectively, *High Noon, Stagecoach* and *My Darling Clementine*. All three films feature the classic Western situation: the town cowed and terrorised by badmen, held in a grip of fear, but liberated at the end by the one superman who's big enough to shoot it out.

Any overlap between this version of events and the true history of the American West is of course purely accidental. But what's interesting in these films is the presentation of the 98.4% of us who aren't supermen or baddies. When Black Jake and his cronies ride into town and kick open the saloon door we tend to gulp our shot of whiskey down and nip out the back. For most of the rest of the flick we skulk in alleyways, shifty-eyed, saying 'But mister, I gotta wife and kids' when anyone asks us to do anything. However, in the last reel, when John Wayne is kicking the crooks in the crutch and restoring Christian civilisation we sidle out gratefully into the sunlight ready for the final scene and the credits, not that we really deserve any. If that's what we're like, no wonder Churchill had to beat the Germans all by himself.

This myth about the way Great Men can take the world by the scruff of the neck and change it is unfortunate in that it contradicts another great myth which says the world never changes – it's always been the same because of Human Nature. This extremely boring myth has been dealt with in earlier sections so hopefully it isn't necessary to have a go at it again. But it's worth noting that it's an idea that fills a lot of the entertainment we're offered.

The film *One Million Years B.C.*, for example, was mainly built around Raquel Welch's breasts but also around the notion that then as now we were all suburban bourgeois *Daily Mail* readers: greedy, centrally concerned about private property, sexually repressed and capable of approximately rational action only when firmly led by one man.

At a jokey level the Flintstones cartoon films push the same idea. Nothing has ever changed. Things have always been the same. Prehistoric man was worried about second hand car values, liked nothing better than hamburger and french fries and was content on a Saturday afternoon to watch the ball game on TV. Meanwhile his good lady wife in the kitchen fluttered about dress patterns and her new hair-do, and the kids, well, heck, they were just kids.

When we break away from these myths flogged by their entertainment industry and turn to the truth the difference is, as usual, complete. When ordinary people – for example, a group of old women from the villages of eastern Nigeria – are asked for once about history, their own history, they are aware of it as progress, as change. Here are some of the things those women said: 'Life these days is more simple and better than the days when I was young'[1]; 'Life has got better this time than my mother's day because civilisation has brought into the world many good changes in life' (p.114); 'Life has completely changed and it is in my opinion better than the days I was born' (p.139); 'Things are different in our days than they were in mother's days. Civilisation has brought in many changes into our lives now. So that we do not have to live in fear and superstition.' (p.146)

So against the myth that things have always been the same we need to throw our knowledge of history as change. Against the myth that change can only come from Great Men we need to place our sense of the things that the rest of us have achieved. We hauled the blocks of stone at Thebes. We rebuilt Babylon. We fought to make the mines safer. And we defeated the Nazis. Armed with a knowledge of our own strength and our own history there are no problems we can't solve, from economic collapse on the one hand to the resurgence of Fascism in Chile on the other.

There's some of that history in a Pete Seeger song called *Talking Union*. It's about the successful fight of

American car workers in 1941 to unionise the Ford factories. The song's typical of the sort of lessons that lie around embedded at all sorts of odd points in our culture, left there as a record of previous struggles. They're there for the taking, to be used in continuing struggles. Here's how the song ends:

> But out in Detroit, here's what they found,
> And out in Pittsburgh, here's what they found,
> And out in Akron, here's what they found,
> And up in Toronto, here's what they found:
> That if you don't let Red-baiting break you up,
> And if you don't let vigilantes break you up,
> And if you don't let race hatred break you up,
> And if you don't let stool-pigeons break you up,
> You'll win . . . what I mean . . .
> Take it easy . . . but take it!

Words from Edith Fowke & Joe Glazer,
Songs of Work and Protest. p.24.

[1] Iris Andreski, *Old Wives' Tales: Life-Stories from Ibibioland*, London 1970, p.79.

Gordon Willis

Kilroy is Here

'Kilroy is Here' is about a man with an aspidistra growing
out of his back; about Kilroy, Felix Grunt and Felicity's
confinement within the oildrum; about the resulting statue
in the public square. Put another way it's about the petty
bourgeoisie, the class struggle and other such matters.

**Pluto Press, Unit 10 Spencer Court,
7 Chalcot Road, London NW1 8LH**

Pluto Plays

Steve Gooch
Female Transport

Six working class women have been convicted of petty
crimes in early nineteenth century London.

'Female Transport' is a tough and realistic account of
their six month voyage to Australia, locked together in a
ship's cell.

From their tentative and desperate first steps in
coming to terms with each other and the oppression of
their all-male jailers, to their final disembarkation as a
tight-knit bunch of hardened rebels at Sydney, the play
shows what effects decisions made above deck produce on
the 'cargo' below.

Steve Gooch
Will Wat, If Not, What Will?

A workshop play about Wat Tyler and the peasant uprising
of 1381. It tells the peasants' side of the story - the side not
normally told in the history books.

The peasants are confronted by Edward III's
militarism, the increasing ambition of the rising merchant
class, the Black Death and the notorious Statute of
Labourers. From spontaneous and almost accidental
beginnings the uprising develops and a leadership gradually
emerges, including Wat Tyler and the lay preacher John
Ball.

Steve Gooch and Paul Thompson
The Motor Show

A play about 60 years of struggle by the working class and
their trade unions against the Ford Motor Company.

'The Motor Show' is an entertaining and political
history of the Ford Empire: from the Model T and the
introduction of the production line, through the slump of
the 1930s and the war, to the industrial battles of recent
years.

Pluto Press, Unit 10 Spencer Court,
7 Chalcot Road, London NW1 8LH